COURSE IN
Isaac Pitman Shorthand

Course in Isaac Pitman Shorthand

A Series of Lessons in

Isaac Pitman's System of Phonography

Revised Edition

NEW YORK
ISAAC PITMAN & SONS, The Phonographic Depot
2 WEST 45TH STREET
and at London, Bath and Melbourne

TORONTO, CANADA
The Commercial Text Book Company
or
The Copp, Clark Co., Limited

1916

Joan Coulter ALCM

COPYRIGHT, 1893, BY ISAAC PITMAN
COPYRIGHT, 1899, BY ISAAC PITMAN & SONS
COPYRIGHT, 1901, BY ISAAC PITMAN & SONS
COPYRIGHT, 1905, BY ISAAC PITMAN & SONS
COPYRIGHT, 1910, BY ISAAC PITMAN & SONS
COPYRIGHT, 1913, BY ISAAC PITMAN & SONS
COPYRIGHT, 1914, BY ISAAC PITMAN & SONS

Printed by J. J. Little & Ives Co.
New York City

CONTENTS

Lesson		Page
1.	Consonants and Second-Place Long Vowels	5
2.	Consonants and First-Place Long Vowels	10
3.	Consonants and Third-Place Long Vowels	14
4.	Short Vowels	19
5.	Diphthongs and Phraseography	23
6.	Review	28
7.	Circle *S* and *Z*	32
8.	Loops *ST* and *STR*	37
9.	Circles *SW* and *SS*	40
10.	Vowel Indication	44
11.	Review	49
12.	Initial Hooks to Straight Strokes	52
13.	Initial Hooks to Curves	55
14.	Initial Hooks to Curves (concluded)	59
15.	Circles and Loops prefixed to Initial Hooks	63
16.	*N* and *F* Hooks	66
17.	Circles and Loops added to Final Hooks	70
18.	Review	74
19.	SHUN Hook	78
20.	SHUN Hook (concluded)	83
21.	Compound Double Consonants	87
22.	Tick and Dot *H*	91
23.	Upward and Downward *L*	96
24.	Upward and Downward *R*	100

CONTENTS

Lesson		Page
25.	Review	104
26.	The Halving Principle	107
27.	The Halving Principle (concluded)	112
28.	The Doubling Principle	117
29.	Vocalization of Double Consonants	122
30.	Diphonic or Two-Vowel Signs	127
31.	Dissyllabic Diphthongs	132
32.	Review	136
33.	Prefixes	138
34.	Suffixes and Terminations	144
35.	Omission of Consonants	149
36.	Figures	153
37.	Compound Words	158
38.	Intersections	162
39.	Distinguishing Vowels	165
40.	Distinguishing Outlines	168
	The Grammalogs and Contractions	173
	Contractions for Names of States and Territories	178
	Fifty Principal Cities arranged according to Population	179
	Grammalogs alphabetically arranged	181
	Contractions alphabetically arranged	184
Phonographic Alphabet		189
	Table of Single and Double Consonants	190
	Phraseograms	191
	Business Correspondence, etc.	195
Appendix—		
	Advanced Speed Practice	209
	Law Phrases	215
	Legal Correspondence	219
Index		237

COURSE IN
ISAAC PITMAN SHORTHAND

LESSON I.

CONSONANTS AND SECOND-PLACE LONG VOWELS.

1. The student must remember that when he is writing shorthand he is to write strictly according to SOUND, leaving out all silent letters. In other words, the spelling in Isaac Pitman Shorthand is *phonetic*, the ordinary spelling being entirely disregarded, and the *sounds* of the words only being represented by the shorthand characters employed. The following examples will illustrate the method to be followed:

Calm would be spelt *k-ah-m,* and would be written

Tomb ,, ,, ,, *t-ōō-m,* ,, ,, ,, ,,

Knee ,, ,, ,, *n-ē* ,, ,, ,, ,,

Door ,, ,, ,, *d-ō-r* ,, ,, ,, ,,

Mail ,, ,, ,, *m-ā-l* ,, ,, ,, ,,

Pole ,, ,, ,, *p-ō-l* ,, ,, ,, ,,

Pier ,, ,, ,, *p-ē-r* ,, ,, ,, ,,

Sew ,, ,, ,, *s-ō* ,, ,, ,, ,,

Meal ,, ,, ,, *m-ē-l* ,, ,, ,, ,,

Name ,, ,, ,, *n-ā-m* ,, ,, ,, ,,

2. In order that the writer may spell phonetically, in accordance with the foregoing directions, he is provided with a sign for every sound in the language. The following eight signs represent the first eight consonants of the phonographic alphabet. The learner will notice that the signs are given in pairs, a light sign and a heavy one; and that the *light sign* represents a *light sound,* while the *heavy sign* represents a *heavy sound*. There is, therefore, a correspondence between the sounds heard and the signs used to represent them. He should copy the signs over and over again, until he knows them thoroughly, and can name and write them with ease. Facility in the use of the shorthand characters will come with practice. The *upright* and *slanting letters* are to be written *downward,* with the ends resting on the ruled line in the writer's note-book. The *horizontal letters* are to be written from *left to right,* and *resting on the line,* as in the examples which follow.

Letter.	Character.	Name.	As in
P	\	pee	ro*p*e, *p*ast, *p*ay
B	\	bee	ro*b*e, *b*oast, *b*ay
T	|	tee	fa*t*e, *t*ip, oa*t*
D	|	dee	fa*d*e, *d*ip, o*d*e
CH	/	chay	et*ch*, *ch*est, *ch*oke
J	/	jay	e*dg*e, *j*est, *j*oke
K	—	kay	lee*k*, *K*ate, pic*k*
G	—	gay	lea*g*ue, *g*ate, pi*g*

SECOND-PLACE LONG VOWELS.

Exercise 1.
Read, copy, and transcribe.

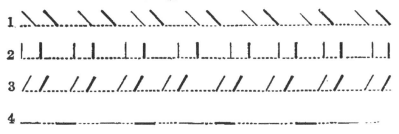

3. Outlines containing two or more consonants should be written without lifting the pen from the paper, a following stroke commencing where the preceding one ends; thus

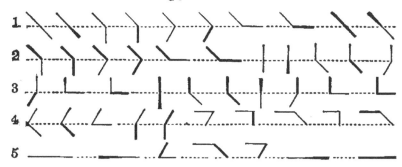

Exercise 2.
Read, copy, and transcribe.

4. The long vowels *ā* and *ō*, as heard in the words *say* and *go*, are represented by a heavy dot and a short, heavy dash respectively. These vowels are called *second-place vowels*, because there are three places for vowels alongside of each consonant stroke, and these two vowels are put in the *middle* or *second* place; as ╲ *pay*, ── *gay*, ┗ *doe*, ── *Co*.

5. A vowel placed at the *left hand side* of an *upright* or *slanting* consonant, or *above* a *horizontal* consonant, is read *before* the consonant; thus ⟍ ape, ⟂ oat, ⟋ age, | oak.

6. A vowel placed at the *right hand side* of an *upright* or *slanting* consonant, or *below* a *horizontal* consonant, is read *after* the consonant; thus ⟍ bay, ⟂ toe, ⟋ jay, — go.

Exercise 3.

Read, copy, and transcribe.

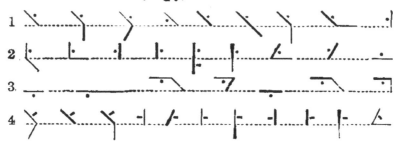

7. The learner will observe that in all the words of the preceding exercise the *first downstroke* rests *on* the line; and that where a downstroke is preceded by a horizontal letter, the latter is written *above* the line, so that the downstroke may rest *on* the line. The position thus indicated is called the *second position*, and the words in the preceding exercise are written in this position because the vowel in each word is a *second-place* vowel. In succeeding exercises, wherever the vowel, or, if there be more than one vowel in the word, the *principal* or distinguishing vowel, is a *second-place* vowel, the outline must be written in the *second position*, as here explained.

8. In shorthand, a small cross (×) is used for a period; the sign ⌒ is employed to express a dash; and other punctuation marks are written as usual. Two

short lines drawn underneath an outline indicate an initial capital; as *Job Cope.*

9. Words of frequent occurrence are expressed in shorthand by one of their letters. A *word* thus abbreviated is called a *grammalog;* the *letter* which is used to represent the whole word is called a *logogram.* The student should learn the grammalogs as thoroughly as possible, because a knowledge of them is necessary in fast writing. Throughout the exercises in this book the grammalogs and contractions are printed in *italic.*

GRAMMALOGS.

a or *an*, *the*, *all*, *too* or *two*, *of*, *to*, *owe* or *Oh!*, *he*, *on*, *but*.

Exercise 4.

Read, copy, and transcribe.

Exercise 5.

Write in Shorthand.

1. Job Day, take *the* cape *to the* boat *to*-day.
2. *He* paid Joe Cope *to* take *the* boat.
3. Take *the* cocoa *to the* page *on the* boat.
4. Joe, *a* joke! Take *an* eight page ode *on* cake *to* Jake *to*-day.
5. Take *the* page *to the* oak.
6. *He* towed *the* boat *to the* oak *to*-day.

LESSON 2.

CONSONANTS AND FIRST-PLACE LONG VOWELS.

10. The next four pairs of consonants are *curves*, and they are written *downward*. They may be joined to each other, or to other consonants, in the same way as the straight letters are joined, a following consonant commencing where a preceding one ends.

Letter.	Character.	Name.	As in
F	⌒	ef	safe, *f*at, lea*f*
V	⌒	vee	sa*v*e, *v*at, lea*v*e
TH	(	ith	wrea*th*, *th*igh, ba*th*
TH	(	thee	wreaTHe, THy, baTHe
S	)	ess	ice, *s*igh, lace
Z	)	zee	oo*z*e, *Z*ion, la*z*y
SH	⌒	ish	a*sh*, *sh*e, la*sh*
ZH	⌒	zhee	mea*s*ure, trea*s*ure, u*s*ual

FIRST-PLACE LONG VOWELS. 11

Exercise 6.

Read, copy, and transcribe.

1 ⌒⌒ ⌒⌒ ⌒⌒ ⌒⌒ ⌒⌒ ⌒⌒
2 ⌒⌒ ⌒⌒ ⌒⌒ ⌒⌒ ⌒⌒ ⌒⌒ ⌒⌒ ⌒⌒
3 ⌒⌒ ⌒⌒ ⌒⌒ ⌒⌒ ⌒⌒ ⌒⌒ ⌒⌒ ⌒⌒
4 ⌒⌒ ⌒⌒ ⌒⌒ ⌒⌒ ⌒⌒

11. The letter *sh* is always written *downward* when standing *alone*, that is, when it is not joined to another letter, as in the preceding exercise; but when it is joined to another letter it may be written *upward*, if the upward form is more convenient. As a rule, it will be found to be more conveniently written *upward* when it immediately precedes ⌒ , ⌒ , ⌒ , ⌒ or ⌒ (*l*); and also when it immediately follows ⌒ , ⌒ , or |
In other cases, it will generally be better to write *sh* *downward*.

Exercise 7.

Read, copy, and transcribe.

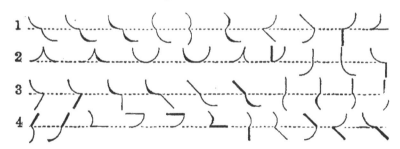

12. The vowels *ah* and *aw*, as heard in the words *pa* and *paw*, are represented by a heavy dot and a short, heavy dash respectively, like the vowels explained in the preceding lesson. The vowels *ah* and *aw*, however, are called *first-place* vowels, because they are put in the *first* vowel place, *i.e.*, at the *beginning* of a consonant; thus ⟍ *pa*, ⟍ *paw*, ⌐ *caw*, ⌐ *auk*.

13. (*a*) The outline of any word containing a *first-place* vowel only, or in which the principal or distinguishing vowel is a *first-place* vowel, is written in the *first position, above* the line; thus ╱ *Shah*.

(*b*) When the word consists of a horizontal letter preceded or followed by an upright or slanting letter, the horizontal letter is raised, so as to allow the upright or slanting letter to occupy the first position; thus ⌐ *talk*.

(*c*) If the word consists of more than one upright or slanting letter, it is the *first* of such letters which must occupy the first position. Note the following examples: ⟍ *baa*, ⌐ *caulk*, ⌐ *cawed*, ⟍ *bought*, ⌐ *daub*.

Exercise 8.

Read, copy, and transcribe.

GRAMMALOGS.

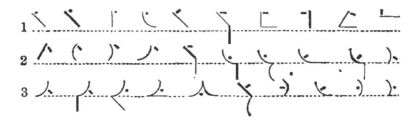
 awe or *ought*, *who*, (up) *and*, (up) *should*, *happy*, *up*, *put*, *by* or *buy*, *be*, *to be*, *at*, *it*, *out*.

FIRST-PLACE LONG VOWELS.

Exercise 9.

Read, copy, and transcribe.

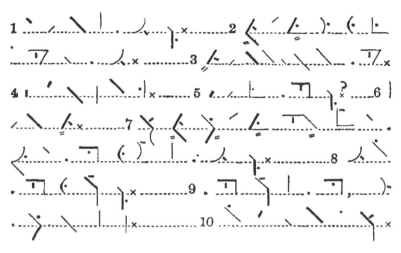

Exercise 10.

Write in Shorthand.

1. Both Joe Cope *and* Jake Page showed *a* goat *at the* show *to-*day.
2. Job, take *the* boat *and put it up by the* gate.
3. *Who* bought *all the* cocoa *to-*day?
4. Pa paid *the* page *to-*day, so *he should be happy.*
5. *Who* saw *the* cape pa bought *at the* show?
6. *It ought to be put on the* coach.
7. They say Job Bate *put all the* folk *on the* boat *and* towed *it to the* bay.

LESSON 3.

CONSONANTS AND THIRD-PLACE LONG VOWELS.

14. The remainder of the consonants are single strokes, not pairs, and they are all *light* signs except ⌣ (*ng*), which is heavy. The three *horizontal letters* ⌢, ⌣, ⌣, are written from *left to right;* ⌠, ⁄, ⁄, ⁄, and ⁄, are written *upward;* and ⟩ and ⟩ are written *downward.*

Letter.	Character.	Name.	As in
M	⌢	em	see*m*, *m*et, chi*m*e
N	⌣	en	see*n*, *n*et, Chi*n*a
NG	⌣	ing	lo*ng*, si*ng*, fa*ng*
L	⌠	el	ta*ll*, *l*ife, mea*l*
R	⟩	ar	a*r*my, a*r*ose, bo*r*e
R	⁄	ray	*r*ate, *r*ogue, *r*ight
W	⁄	way	*w*ade, a*w*are, *w*eep
Y	⁄	yay	*Y*ale, *y*oke, *y*ore
H	⁄	hay	*h*ope, ad*h*ere, *h*urry
H	⟩	hay	*h*igh, *h*ew, *h*ook

THIRD-PLACE LONG VOWELS.

Exercise 11.

Read, copy, and transcribe.

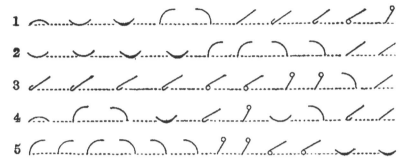

15. The consonants R and H are each provided with two forms, an upstroke and a downstroke. This is for convenience of joining to other consonants, and also for the purpose of *vowel indication* in fast writing. The rules governing the use of these forms will be fully explained in a later lesson, but, meanwhile, the following brief statement will be useful:

(*a*) Downward R is written before *m*, as ⟋⟍ *roam*, but, with this exception, when a word *begins* with the sound of R, or *ends* with R and a *sounded vowel*, the upward form is used; as ⟋ *ray*, ⟋⎯ *rogue*, ⟍⟋ *Pharaoh*.

(*b*) When a word *begins* with a vowel followed by R, or *ends* with the sound of R, the-*downward* form is used; as ⟍ *air*, ⟍ *ore*, ⟍ *fare*.

(*c*) The *upward* form of H is used, *except* when H *stands alone* or is followed by ⎯ or ⎯ ; as ⟋ *hay*, ⟋ *hawk*, ⟋ *Hague*.

16. The consonants of the last group are joined to one another, and to other consonants, in the manner already explained with regard to the letters previously treated.

Exercise 12.

Read, copy, and transcribe.

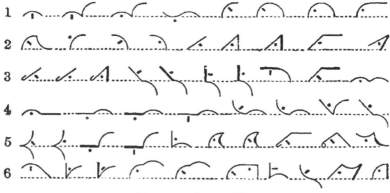

Exercise 13.

Write in Shorthand.

1. May they *all* take *a* share *at the* game?
2. Mail *the* bale *of* tape *to* Hague *and* Hay *to*-day.
3. Take *all the* coal *by* boat *to*-day.
4. *Put up a* loaf; *be out by* four; *and* take *the* coach *at the* gate.
5. Paul *and* Jake may *be at the* shore.
6. They *should all be out by* four.

17. The vowels ē and o͞o, as heard in the words *keep* and *cool*, are expressed, like the vowels already explained, by a heavy dot and a short heavy dash respectively. They are called *third-place* vowels, because they are written in the third vowel place, *i.e.*, at the *end* of a consonant; thus ___|___ tea, ___⌒___ loo, ___⌐___ fee, _____ eke.

18. (a) The outline of any word in which the vowel, or the principal or distinguishing vowel, is a *third-place* vowel, must be written in the *third position, through* the line; and when the outline of the word consists of an upright or slanting letter immediately preceded or followed by a horizontal letter, the latter is *lowered*, so

THIRD-PLACE LONG VOWELS. 17

that the upright or slanting letter may be written through the line; thus ⟿ *keep,* ⟿ *keyed,* ⟿ *move,* ⟿ *cool,* ⟿ *peach,* ⟿ *teach,* ⟿ *eve,* ⟿ *rue.*

(*b*) It will be seen, therefore, that the *first upright or slanting letter* in an outline must occupy the position as required by the principal vowel in the word, the other letters being raised or lowered accordingly.

(*c*) There is, however, *no third position* for words whose outlines consist of horizontal letters only. When the vowel or principal vowel in such words is a *third-place* vowel, the outline is written in the second position, *on the line;* thus ⟿ *meek.*

19. When a *third-place* vowel occurs *between two strokes*, it is written *before the second stroke*, as in the preceding examples.

Exercise 14.

Read, copy, and transcribe.

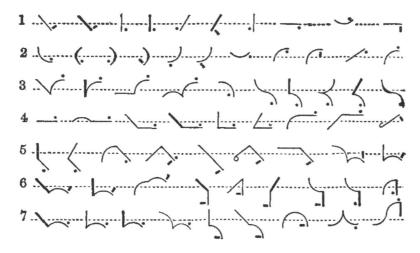

2 *S. C.*

GRAMMALOGS.

_..|.._ had, |_ do, _..|.._ different or difference, _../_ much, _/_ which, _../_ each, _../_ large, _——_ can, _—_ come, _——_ go or ago, _—_ give or given.

Exercise 15.

Read, copy, and transcribe.

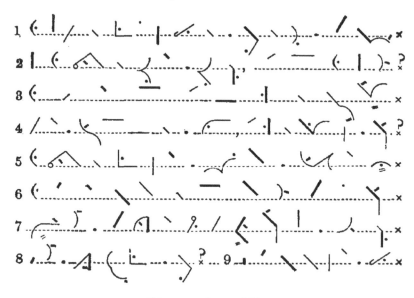

Exercise 16.

Write in Shorthand.

1. *Which* way *should* they *go to* reach *the* pool?
2. *Do* they read *a different* page *to*-day?
3. *He* may *go by the* coach, *and* take *the* boat *at the* pier.
4. *Go,* Joe Booth, *and* show *the* poor page *the difference.*
5. *He should be on the* road *by* four.
6. They *had to go a different* way *at* sea.
7. They fear they may *be out of the* way.
8. Leave *a large* share *of the* food *on the* boat; *it* may make *much difference to* Joe Shaw.

LESSON 4.

SHORT VOWELS.

20. The *short* vowels, ă, ĕ, ĭ, ŏ, ŭ, o͝o, as heard in the words "*Thăt pĕn ĭs nŏt mŭch go͝od,*" are expressed by dots and short dashes similar to those employed for the representation of the long vowels already explained; but the signs for the *short* vowels are made *light*, in order to show the short, or light, sounds of the vowels.

21. The short vowels, like the long vowels, are named according to the position they occupy with regard to a stroke consonant. Thus ă, ĕ, ĭ, are called respectively *first-place*, *second-place*, and *third-place* vowels; while ŏ, ŭ, o͝o, are also, in the order given, *first-place*, *second-place*, and *third-place* vowels. Note the following examples: ⌐ băt, ⌐ bĕt, ⌐ bĭt, ⌐ lŏck, ⌐ lŭck, ⌐ lo͝ok.

22. *All first-place* vowels and *second-place* vowels, whether *long or short*, occurring between two strokes, are written *after the first stroke*. *All third-place* vowels, whether *long or short*, occurring between two strokes, are written *before the second stroke*. Note the following pairs of words: bale, bell; raid, red; fade, fed; date, debt; roam, rum; robe, rub; goal, gull; shade, shed; keel, kill; leave, live; peak, pick; meal, mill; heed, hid.

23. The rules for the position of outlines of words containing short vowels are exactly the same as those

20 COURSE IN ISAAC PITMAN SHORTHAND.

governing the position of words containing long vowels. For example: 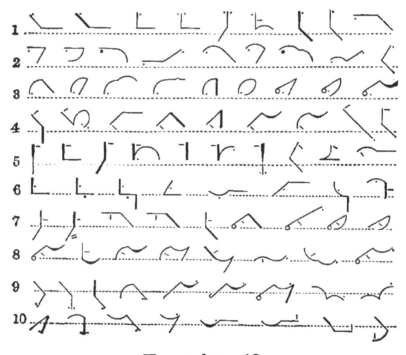 *palm*, *pack*; *bake*, *beck*; *deem*, *dim*; *wrought*, *rot*; *coal*, *cull*; *pool*, *pull*.

Exercise 17.

Read, copy, and transcribe.

Exercise 18.

Write in Shorthand.

1. Pack *the* bag *and* take *it to the* gig *at* four.
2. Ask Jim *to* fetch *the* check book, *and put it on the* ledge.
3. Take *the* money, *and buy a* jar *of* ink.
4. They may *all go to the* dock *and* see *the* ship off.

SHORT VOWELS. 21

5. Ask Tom *to be* awake *and* ready *to go on to the* ship *by* four.
6. Hurry *up*, Jack Murray, *and* carry *all the* baggage *to the* hotel.
7. *The happy* fellow rowed away *to the* ship.
8. *Do* they *owe a* debt *to* Adam Bailey?
9. Ask Kitty Webb *to* take *a* dollar *out of the* bag, *and go and buy the* calico.
10. They may *all go on* Monday *to* see *the* game *of* golf.
11. May they take *a* share *of the* sherry *to* poor Jim King?
12. They *go by the* ship "Carrie," *and* they hope *to be* back *by the* fourth *of* March.

GRAMMALOGS.

⌇ half, ⌇ if, ⌇ have, ⌇ thank-ed, (think, (youth, ⌇ though, (them or they.

Exercise 19.

Read, copy, and transcribe.

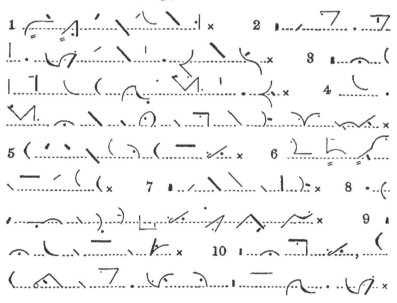

Exercise 20.

Write in Shorthand.

1. *They think they* may *have to go to the* bank *and* cash a check *to* pay *the youth the* money.
2. *The youth* may *be happy if they* pay *half the* bill.
3. *Though they go out on the* tenth, *they* may *come* back *by* an early mail.
4. *Who can* envy *them if they have to* take *the* shabby coach back *to*-morrow?
5. *They should* take *the* keg *to the* back *of the* shed.
6. *He* came back *to them a* month *ago.*
7. *They have to go and thank the* judge *to*-day.
8. Ask *the youth to* take *the* canoe *and* fetch *the* fish.
9. *They think the* lad *may have to go to* Canada.
10. *Half the* party came *to give a* vote *each to* Adam Bailey.

LESSON 5.

DIPHTHONGS AND PHRASEOGRAPHY.

24. The four diphthongs, *ī, ow, oi,* and *ū,* as heard in the words *bite, cow, boil,* and *few,* are expressed as follows:

ī,   ʌ *ow,*   *oi,*   ∩ *ū.*

25. The diphthongs *i* and *oi* are written in the *first* vowel-place, at the *beginning* of a stroke; and, therefore, the outlines of words in which either of these is the only or principal vowel-sound are placed in the first position, *above* the line; thus *boy, boil, boiler, coy, decoy, coil.*

26. The diphthongs *u* and *ow* are written in the *third* vowel-place, at the *end* of a stroke; and, therefore, the outlines of words in which either of these is the only or principal vowel-sound are placed in the third position, *through* the line; thus *purely, purity, purify, cube, cubic, rout, bout, allow, allowed.*

27. A small tick, upward or downward, attached to a diphthong-sign expresses any short vowel; thus *diary, dial, piety, loyalty, vowel, manual, riot.* The sign representing a diphthong and vowel is called a *triphone.*

28. (a) The diphthong ī may be joined initially to a downstroke, as ⟋ item, ⟋ ice.

(b) The diphthongs ow and oi may be joined initially to upward l, as ⟋ owlish, ⟋ oiling.

(c) The diphthongs ow and ū may be joined finally to a downstroke, as ⟋ bough, ⟋ due.

(d) The diphthongs ū, ow, and ī, may be joined to the consonants k, g, m, n, and l (up), thus ⟋ cue, ⟋ argue, ⟋ renew, ⟋ value, ⟋ now, ⟋ nigh.

Exercise 21.

Read, copy, and transcribe.

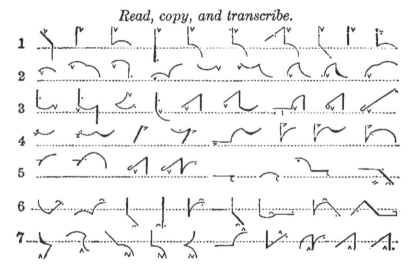

Exercise 22.

Write in Shorthand.

1. *Do they* know *of the* failure *of* Hugh Riley?
2. *All the* folk *think and* say *he should* retire *by* July.
3. *The* tide may wash away *the* dike *by* five.

4. *Should the* envoy *come out to-*day *he* may enjoy *a* ride *to* Albany.

5. *The* puny deputy duly came *and* valued *the* couch.

6. *They had to* show *the* check *given them by* Tom Lloyd.

7. *The* lively dealer took *a* widely *different* view *of the* affair *to-*day.

8. *If they* deny my right *to go out on the* tenth, *they* may *all* rue *it*.

9. *They* assume *a large* share *of the* duty; *but they have* no right *to it, and they* may *have to give it up*.

10. Pursue *a* life *of* purity, *and* so rebuke *them*.

11. *They should* decoy *the* rowdy fellow *to the* review, *and* leave *the* rogue *to* enjoy *the* air.

12. *If they* take refuge *on the* boat, *they can* defy *the* power *of the* enemy *to* take *them* or *to* move *them* away.

GRAMMALOGS.

I or *eye*, how, *why*, *ay* (yes), *beyond*, *you*, *with*, *when*, *what*, *would*.

29. Longhand writers often join words together without lifting the pen from the paper. The same may be done in shorthand. The practice of joining words in this way is called *Phraseography*, and the words thus joined make a *Phraseogram*. The first word of a phraseogram (generally a grammalog) should occupy the position which it would occupy if it stood alone. Thus, a phraseogram commencing with *I* should commence above the line, because *I*, as a logogram, is written above the line, as *I have*, *I think*, *I say*. A first position logogram, however, may be slightly lowered or raised to permit of the following

word being written through or over the line; as _I see_, _with much_. A phraseogram beginning with *you* should begin on the line, because *you*, as a logogram, is written on the line when it stands alone; thus _you may_, _you should be_. When joined to ⌢, ⌒, or —, the sign _may be_ shortened to _; thus _(I'm = I am)_, _(I'll = I will)_ _I can_. The vowel should be inserted in the phraseogram _to go_.

The following examples of phraseograms should be carefully read and copied by the learner.

PHRASEOGRAMS.

	I have		how can they
	I have had		why do you
	I will		why have you
	I will be		you can
	I am		with much
	I may be		with which
	I may		with each
	I thank you		when they
	I think you should be		what do you
	you will		what may be
	you will be		what can be
	you may be		it would be
	if you should be		and if you should be

Exercise 23.

Read, copy, and transcribe.

[shorthand exercises 1–14]

Exercise 24.

The *phrases* in this and following exercises are indicated by the *hyphen*.

Write in Shorthand.

1. *Do-you* think *you-can* rely *on-them to-*take *all the* money *to the* bank *to-*day?
2. *Why-do-you* ask *the* poor *youth to-*ride *the* lame mule?
3. *If-you-should-be* back *by* five, *I-may come and* see *you.*
4. *I-think I-*am likely *to be* away *by the* time *you* get back.
5. *I-think-you-should* ask *them to-*take *the* oil back.
6. *Why-do-you* assume *the* right *to* argue *with* so shabby *a* fellow?
7. *I-think-you-should* write *them, if-you* think *you-can-do* what *they* ask *you to-do.*
8. *How-can-they* ask *you to-*go *to* Ithaca *to-*morrow?
9. *I-think I-*may guarantee *the* tube *to be all-they* say.
10. *I-may-be* wrong, *but I-think I-*am right.

LESSON 6.

REVIEW.

30. In this lesson the learner is asked to review the rules set forth in the preceding pages; to learn eight more grammalogs; and to practise those he has already learned.

31. The preceding rules may be briefly summarized as follows:

(a) Isaac Pitman Shorthand is *phonetic*, the *spelling* being by *sound*.

(b) There are *twelve vowels*, expressed by dots and dashes, and written in *three places*, above, below, or by the side of consonants.

(c) There are *three positions* for writing outlines, and the position of a word is governed by its vowel, or principal vowel.

(d) There are *four* double vowels or *diphthongs*.

(e) There are *two* forms *each* for R and H, the alternatives being provided for easy joinings and for vowel indication.

(f) Words of frequent occurrence are expressed by one of their letters. Such words are called *grammalogs*.

(g) *Phraseography* is the name given to the principle of joining *words* together.

REVIEW. 29

GRAMMALOGUES.

saw, so or us, see, sea, was, whose, shall, wish, usual-ly.

Exercise 25.

Read, copy, and transcribe.

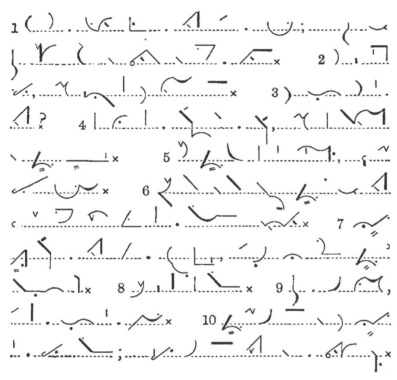

Exercise 26.

Write in Shorthand.

1. *Do-you* know *the* name *of the* ship lying **out by the** buoy?
2. *I-think it-was on the* fourth *of* July *he* came **to see us**.
3. *I-think I-saw* the youth go out *a* minute *ago*.

4. *You* appear *to-have a* fear *of the large youth who* came to *us at the* farm.
5. *To be of* value *ought to be the wish of each of you.*
6. *I-wish I-had given the* rod away ere *the* thief took *it.*
7. *Do-you* know *whose it-can-be ?*
8. *Why should-they* say *I*-am *out ?*
9. *What difference can-it* make *to-you if I-have to-go out by the* tenth?
10. *I-see-you* know *two of-them.*

Exercise 27.

Read, copy, and transcribe.

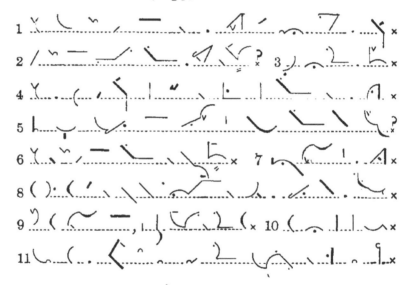

Exercise 28.

Write in Shorthand.

1. *I-shall-be happy to-have-you do-so if-you-can* manage *it.*
2. *Do-you think* he knew *the difference ?*
3. *I-think-so ;* but *I*-will ask *the* fellow.
4. *If-they* go out, *I-think-you and-I* may *go out too.*

REVIEW. 31

5. *Though they-may say no, I-know it shall-be different.*
6. *I-think it-was usual to-give it to-each of-them.*
7. *You and-I usually go all the way by the sea.*
8. *I-think the new book may-be of value to us now.*
9. *If-you-like to-give them a copy, they-may-be happy to read it.*
10. *They thanked the youth who carried the baggage to the ship, and he-was happy.*

Exercise 29.

Read, copy, and transcribe.

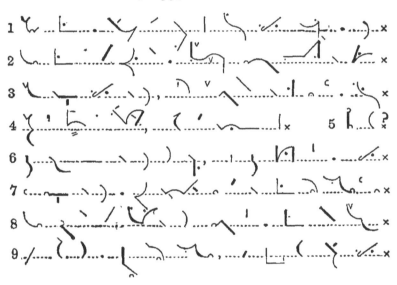

LESSON 7.

CIRCLE *S* AND *Z*.

32. The sounds of *s* and *z* are two of the most frequently occurring sounds in the language, and it is, therefore, necessary that they should be provided with very easily written signs. The student has learned that the sign) expresses *s*, and that the sign) expresses *z*. These sounds, however, are also represented by a *small circle*, which is easily written and at the same time joins readily with the various stroke consonants.

33. When the circle *stands alone*, or is joined to *straight consonants* not forming an angle, it is written in the direction *opposite* to that in which the hands of a clock move round; thus ⟟ ⟟ *sp*, ⟟ *ps*, ⟟ *psp*, ⟟ *st*, ⟟ *ts*, ⟟ *tst*, ⟟ *sch*, ⟟ *chs*, ⟟ *sk*, ⟟ *ks*, ⟟ *ksk*, ⟟ *sr*, ⟟ *rs*, ⟟ *rsr*.

34. When the circle occurs between two straight strokes *forming an angle*, it is written *outside the angle*; thus ⟟ *bsch*, ⟟ *tsp*, ⟟ *jsp*, ⟟ *ksp*, ⟟ *ksr*, ⟟ *rsk*.

35. When joined to *curved letters*, the circle is written *inside the curve;* and when it occurs *between two curves* it is usually written *inside the first curve;* thus ⟟ *sf*, ⟟ *fs*, ⟟ *fsf*, ⟟ *ss*, ⟟ *ss*, ⟟ *ssr*, ⟟ *sm*, ⟟ *sms*, ⟟ *rsn*, ⟟ *ksn*, ⟟ *nsk*, ⟟ *msr*, ⟟ *sl*, ⟟ *sls*, ⟟ *slsr*, ⟟ *ssh*, ⟟ *sshs*, ⟟ *msv*.

CIRCLE "S" AND "Z."

36. The circle *s* is always read *first* at the *beginning* of a word, and *last* at the *end* of a word; thus ⌐ *eat*, ⌐ *seat*, ⌐ *seats;* ⌐ *tow*, ⌐ *stow*, ⌐ *stows;* ⌐ *eke*, ⌐ *seek*, ⌐ *seeks;* ⌐ *oar*, ⌐ *soar*, ⌐ *soars;* ⌐ *suppose*, ⌐ *cities*, ⌐ *series*.

37. At the *end* of a stroke, or in the *middle* of a word, the circle may be used to express *either s* or *z;* but at the *beginning* of a word it can be used to express the *light* sound of *s* only; as ⌐ *race*, ⌐ *rose*, ⌐ *racer*, ⌐ *raising;* ⌐ *sorrow*, ⌐ *zero;* ⌐ *seal*, ⌐ *zeal*.

Exercise 30.
Read, copy, and transcribe.

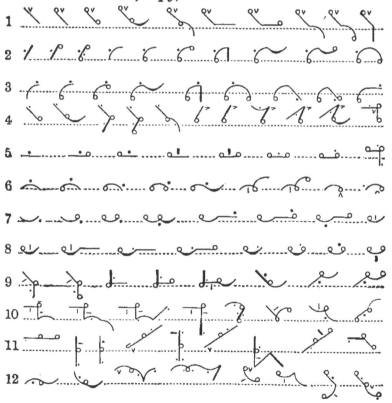

Exercise 31.

Write in Shorthand.

1. Soap, soups, stew, side, such, spares, spokes.
2. Seeds, schemes, spoils, skips, scoop, speed.
3. Safes, south, slow, solo, soon, smokes, mice.
4. Smith, snaps, sold, snares, smacks, solids.
5. Sky, scares, spades, signs, designs, dies.
6. Face, voice, revise, canvas, bonus, police.
7. Atlas, tusk, risks, bestows, rasps, gossip.
8. Chosen, visits, masks, resumes, desires, pacifies.
9. Tuesday, Wednesday, deceit, tacit, nonsense.
10. Sykes, stay, sums, sinews, maxims, abuse.

38. When the stroke ⌒ precedes a circle and curve, or follows a curve and circle, it is written in the *same direction* as the *circle;* thus ⌒ lessen, ⌒ Lawson, ⌒ lesser, ⌒ toilsome, ⌒ vessel, ⌒ thistle, ⌒ cancel, ⌒ muscle.

39. The word *the,* which is represented by a light dot on the line, is also expressed by a light, slanting *tick,* joined to the preceding character, and written either upward or downward, in the direction which will give the sharper angle; thus ⌒ of the, > to the, ⌒ and the, ⌒ should the, ⌒ I think the, ⌒ I have the, ⌒ with the, ⌒ when the, ⌒ he is the, ⌒ it is the, ⌒ is the, ⌒ as the or *has the.* The first stroke of ⌒ *on the* must be written slanting, in order that it may not clash with ⌒ I. The tick *the* can *never* be used at the *beginning* of a word or sentence.

GRAMMALOGS.

⌒ as or has, ○ is or his, ⌒ because, ⌒ itself, ⌒ those, ⌒ this, ⌒ these or thus, ⌒ myself, ⌒ himself, ⌒ me or my, ⌒ him or may, / are, ⌒ our or hour, ⌒ we.

CIRCLE "S" AND "Z."

Exercise 32.

Read, copy, and transcribe.

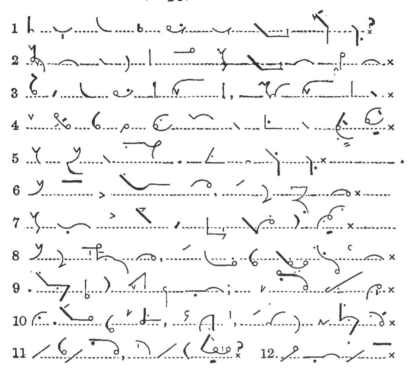

Exercise 33.

Write in Shorthand.

Sir:

Those silks *you* spoke *of* came *to-this* office *to*-day, *and-I-shall* thus *be* ready *to* show *them to-my* customer *on*-Wednesday. *He-comes himself to see me, because he-has to* pass *my* office *on-his* way *to-the* depot. *He-is a large buyer. I-myself had* business dealings *with him a* long time *ago.* The silk *itself is all*-right; *the* designs *are* nice; *and so I* hope *to-do a* big business *with our* new shades.

Yours,

Exercise 34.

Read, copy, and transcribe.

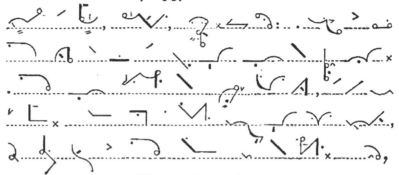

Exercise 35.

Write in Shorthand.

Sirs:

We-are in receipt *of*-yours *of*-May 4th, advising *us of-the* dispatch *of-the* six dozen silk parasols, *and-we* hope *to*-receive *these* in *a* few days' time. *Our* customers *are* feeling some annoyance *at-the* delay, *and-we* fear *we-are* losing business. *If-you-are*-now ready *with-the* new season's designs in ladies' capes *and* costumes, *we should* like *to see them*.

Yours,

LESSON 8.
LOOPS *ST* AND *STR*.

40. A *small loop*, half the length of the stroke to which it is attached, represents *st*; thus ⁀ *ache*, ⁀ *stake*, ⁀ *stale*, ⁀ *store*, ⁀ *stout*. When written at the *beginning* of a stroke the loop represents *st only*; but when written at the *end* of a stroke it represents *either st or zd*; thus ⁀ *coast*, ⁀ *accused*, ⁀ *mist*, ⁀ *amused*. The loop may also be used *medially*, when convenient; thus ⁀ *justify*, ⁀ *toasting*.

41. A *large loop*, two-thirds the length of the stroke to which it is attached, represents *str*; thus ⁀ *poster*, ⁀ *luster*. The *str* (ster) loop must *not* be written at the *beginning* of a word; but it may be employed *medially*, as in ⁀ *masterpiece*. The circle *s* may be added to the loops, thus ⁀ *coasts*, ⁀ *masts*, ⁀ *posters*, ⁀ *lusters*.

42. The loops *st* (stee) and *str* (ster) follow the *same rule* of writing as the *circle s*; that is, they are written with a *backward* motion (in the *opposite* direction to that taken by the hands of a clock) when attached to *straight* letters, and *inside curves*. The loops also follow the *same rule* of reading as the *circle s*; so that the loop *st* is always read *first* at the *beginning* of a word, and *last* at the *end* of a word; while the loop *str* (which is never used initially) is always read *last* at the *end* of a word.

43. The following examples will show the similarity between the rules for circle *s* and for the loops *st* and *str*; thus ⁀ *pass*, ⁀ *past*, ⁀ *pastor*, ⁀ *pastors*; ⁀ *soup*, ⁀ *stoop*; ⁀ *seal*, ⁀ *steal*; ⁀ *mass*, ⁀ *mast*, ⁀ *master*, ⁀ *masters*.

44. The vowel *aw* may be joined initially to upward *l* as ⌒ *awl* ⌒ *also;* and the logogram ⌒ *aw (all)* may be joined in compound words like ⌒ *almost,* ⌒ *already,* ⌒ *all-wise.*

Exercise 36.
Read, copy, and transcribe.

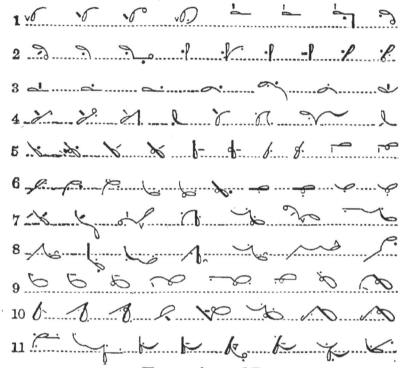

Exercise 37.
Write in Shorthand.

1. Rusts, mast, mist, paced, raced, faced, best.
2. Stab, steal, sting, stop, stoop, star, stark, stale.
3. Stung, stinging, stoves, steer, west, waste, wastes.
4. Past, pests, tossed, jests, fused, sneezed.
5. Voiced, rejoiced, amassed, August, spaced.
6. Reposed, dismissed, fastest, advised, revised.
7. Chester, Manchester, musters, ministers.
8. Tasters, coasters, feasters, Bagster, Dexter.

LOOPS "ST" AND "STR."

GRAMMALOGUES.

first, most, must, influence, influenced, next, in or any, no or know, own, suggest-ed.

Exercise 38.
Read, copy, and transcribe.

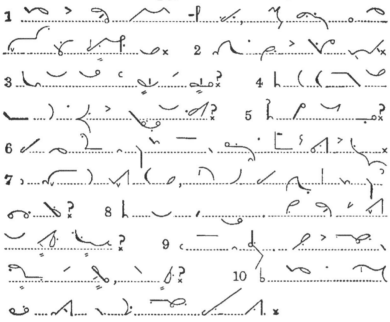

Exercise 39.
Write in Shorthand.

Sir: *The* names *of-the* vessels *are-the* "Star" *and-the* "Chester." *The* "Chester" *goes out on*-Wednesday *next, the first of* July, *and-is most* likely *to*-reach Adelaide *by-the first of* August. She *has usually a* heavy cargo *on-the* passage *out. If-you*-will-*be influenced by our* advice, *you*-will book *a* passage *by-this* vessel *to*-day. *You-must own you have-no*-time *to*-waste *if-you-are to* be *in*-time *to influ*ence Webster *and* Staveley. *The* last *of-the* bales *was* invoiced *to*-day. *The* rest *of-the* business *can-be* discussed *when you-come to-the* office. Yours,

LESSON 9.
CIRCLES *SW* AND *SS*.

45. A *large circle* at the *beginning* of a stroke represents *sw*, as ⟨⟩ *sweep*, ⟨⟩ *swim*, ⟨⟩ *switch;* and a *large circle* at the *end* of a stroke represents the light or heavy sound of *ss*, as ⟨⟩ *paces*, ⟨⟩ *raises*, ⟨⟩ *faces*, ⟨⟩ *causes*.

46. The circles *sw* (*sway*) and *ss* (*ses*) are written in the same direction as the circle *s*. The *sway* circle can be written *only* at the *beginning* of a word, as ⟨⟩ *sweet;* but the *ses* circle may be written in the *middle* or at the *end* of a word; thus ⟨⟩ *necessity*, ⟨⟩ *nieces*, ⟨⟩ *excessive*, ⟨⟩ *cases*.

47. When a vowel *other* than short *ĕ* occurs between the consonants represented by the large medial or final circle, the vowel sign may be placed within the circle; thus ⟨⟩ *insist*, ⟨⟩ *exercise*, ⟨⟩ *exercises*, ⟨⟩ *Colossus*.

48. (*a*) The *sw* circle is employed in *phrasing* to express the words *as we;* thus ⟨⟩ *as we have*, ⟨⟩ *as we think*, ⟨⟩ *as we can*. It is also used in the phrase ⟨⟩ *as well as*.

(*b*) The *ss* circle is employed in *phrasing* to express the *two s's* in such phrases as ⟨⟩ *this is*, ⟨⟩ *it is said*, ⟨⟩ *as soon as*, ⟨⟩ *in this city*.

(*c*) The circle *s* may be used instead of the *st* loop in phrases like ⟨⟩ *it must be*, ⟨⟩ *you must receive*, ⟨⟩ *last time*, ⟨⟩ *next time*.

CIRCLES "SW" AND "SS."

49. To avoid an awkward outline, the upward ╱ is written, whether there is a final vowel or not, when *r* follows a straight upstroke, or *ks* or *gs*, or a curve and circle like ⌒ or ⌒ ; thus ⟋ *were*, ⟋ *weary*, ⟋ *Kaiser*, ⟋ *geyser*, ⟋ *officer*, ⟋ *viscera*, ⟋ *answer*, ⟋ *necessary*.

Exercise 40.

Read, copy, and transcribe.

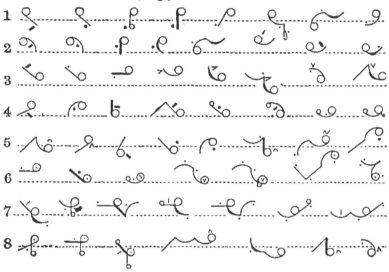

Exercise 41.

Write in Shorthand.

1. *It-is*-said *the* ship Swallow *is to*-sail *on* Tuesday; *but-this-is* wrong *as-we-know* she-*is* still *in* ballast.
2. *As-we-have*-said, *she-is the* swiftest, *as*-well-*as-the* biggest, steamer *they own*.
3. *As-we-can* easily ship *all-the* cases *to*-morrow, *you-must*-*be* ready *to*-mail *all-the* invoices.
4. *You-must* emphasize *the* necessity *of-the* case, *and* see *to-the* boxes being ready *in*-time.

42 COURSE IN ISAAC PITMAN SHORTHAND.

5. *It-is*-said *he* refuses *to-give us-the* allowances *on-the* pieces *of* silk.
6. *If-he* chooses *to*-resist *us, what-can-they* do *with-the* pieces?
7. *They-may* insist *on* refusing-*the* laces *because of-the* excessive charges, *and may* ask *us to* change them *as-soon-as-they* know-*the* cost.
8. *You-must*-receive *a* check, same *as* last-time.

GRAMMALOGUES.

... *as is*, ○ *is as*, ⌒ *this is* or *themselves*, ⌒ *ourselves*, ⌐ *special-ly*, ⌐ *speak*, ⌒ *several*, ⌒ *yes*, ⌐ *high*, ⌐ *house*, ⌒ *we, way*.

Exercise 42.
Read, copy, and transcribe.

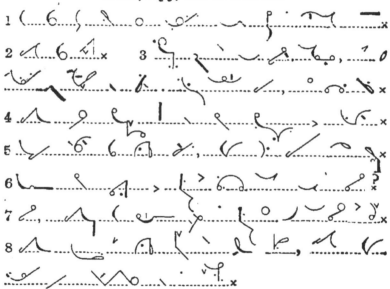

Exercise 43.
Write in Shorthand.

1. *Do-you* know *if-they* themselves have sold-*the* switch *to-the* new firm, *as-is* said *to* be-*the* case?

CIRCLES "SW" AND "SS." 43

2. *Yes, we-have ourselves* seen *several of-the* switches *in* use, *and-we-have special* reasons *to*-suppose *the* fact *to be as you* state.
3. *We-are specially* desirous *of-having-the* new Benson steel tubes *put to a test, and-we-think* Benson's themselves should see-the test, so they-may see-the fact is-as we say it-is.
4. *I*-will *speak to-the* head *of-the* firm, *and suggest a* test *the next*-time *I*-am-*in-the*-city.

Exercise 44.
Read, copy, and transcribe.

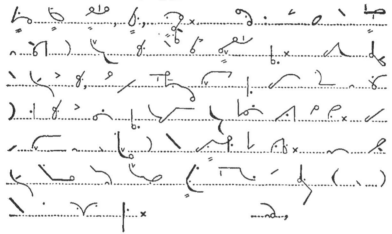

Exercise 45.
Write in Shorthand.

Swan & Lester,
      Kansas City, Mo.
Sirs:

    We-have a special sale *of* essences *and* sweet syrups *to*-day, *as-it-is* necessary *to* dispose *of*-some *of-our* stock. *As-we-know* just *what you* use, *we-can, if-you*-like, select *a* dozen cases *and* set *them* aside, *and you-can* take same *as*-soon-*as you-are* ready. *How*-many *shall we* set aside? *Shall we* ship *you a* dozen *specially* nice cases?

                  Yours sincerely,

LESSON 10.

VOWEL INDICATION.

50. A vowel cannot be read *before* an initial circle or loop (see paragraphs 36, 42, 46). It follows, therefore, that when a word *begins* or *ends* with a vowel, a *stroke* consonant must be employed, and not a circle or loop; thus ⟋ *ask,* ⟋ *assail,* ⟋ *asleep,* ⟋ *rosy,* ⟋ *daisy,* ⟋ *dusty,* ⟋ *honesty.* Compare these words with ⟋ *sack,* ⟋ *sail,* ⟋ *sleep* ⟋ *rose,* ⟋ *days,* ⟋ *dust,* ⟋ *honest.*

51. A vowel cannot be shown *between the letters* expressed by a *loop.* The *separate* letters, therefore, and not a loop, must be written in such words as ⟋ *beset,* ⟋ *tacit,* ⟋ *reside,* ⟋ *pasture,* ⟋ *visitor.* Compare these words with ⟋ *best,* ⟋ *taste,* ⟋ *raised,* ⟋ *pastor,* ⟋ *investor.*

52. The stroke *s* is written at the *beginning* of a word when *s* and a vowel *form a syllable* and are followed by *another vowel,* or by *s* or *z;* thus ⟋ *science,* ⟋ *Siam,* ⟋ *sighing,* ⟋ *saucer.*

53. The stroke *s* is written at the *end* of a word when the syllable *-ous* is immediately preceded by a diphthong; as ⟋ *tortuous,* ⟋ *joyous.*

54. The stroke *s* is retained in compound words like ⟋ *saw-mill,* ⟋ *saw-dust,* ⟋ *sea-beach,* ⟋ *sea-gull.*

55. It will be seen from the foregoing rules, and from the rules for writing R (paragraph 15), that the *outline*

VOWEL INDICATION.

of a word frequently indicates the *presence* or *absence of a vowel*, and that, therefore, the writer may safely omit an initial or final vowel in very many words. Thus, he need not insert the initial vowel in words like ⎯⎯ *ask*, ⎯⎯ *assume*, ⎯⎯ *arise*, because the outline in each case *indicates* a preceding vowel. Nor need he insert the final vowel in such words as ⎯⎯ *rusty*, ⎯⎯ *policy*, ⎯⎯ *carry*, ⎯⎯ *summary*, because the outline *indicates* a final vowel in such words.

56. An *unaccented short vowel*, in the middle of a word, may usually be omitted; thus ⎯⎯ *absence*, ⎯⎯ *business*, ⎯⎯ *customer*, ⎯⎯ *resign*, ⎯⎯ *delayed*, ⎯⎯ *officer*, ⎯⎯ *disposal*.

Exercise 46.
Read, copy, and transcribe.

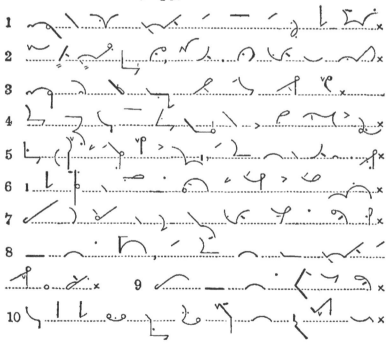

Exercise 47.

Write in Shorthand.

Sir:

When can you ship *us-the* acid *we* bought last-month? *You* said *we should-have-it by* Wednesday the 10th *at-the* latest. *We-are as* busy *as-we-can-be* just-now, *and-the* delay *is* causing *much* annoyance *to-our* customers, *as-well-as* loss *to-ourselves*. Are *you* uneasy *as-to-the* bill? *If so, we can* mail *you* check *on* receipt *of-the* invoice. *We* rely *on-you to* ship *the* stuff *by an* early steamer, *and-we* assume *you*-will write *us to*-morrow.

Yours,

Grammalogs and Contractions.

language or owing, thing, young, anything, nothing, something, or, your, year, New York.

Phraseograms.

I am sorry, we are sorry, you may as well, yours respectfully, respectfully yours.

Exercise 48.

Read, copy, and transcribe.

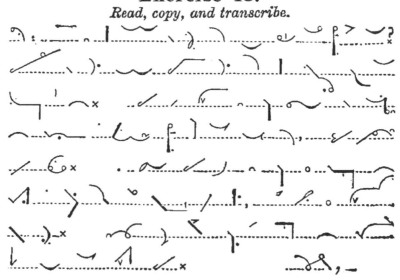

VOWEL INDICATION.

Exercise 49.

Write in Shorthand.

1. *I-am*-sorry *I-can-do* nothing *to* assist *the* Society just-now.
2. *You-may-as*-well take *up-the language* now *as next year.*
3. *If-you-are to*-make *anything of-yourself, you*-will-*have to-do-something this year.*
4. *Have-you* seen-*the* new *house which* Robson *has* bought *by-the* beach?
5. *I-think it-was an* unwise *thing to buy so large a house* just-now.
6. *What* does *young* Jackson say?
7. Does *he think it-was a* wise *thing to-do?*
8. *We-are*-sorry *to* see Jackson *is to*-leave-*the* city *next year.*

Exercise 50.

Read, copy, and transcribe.

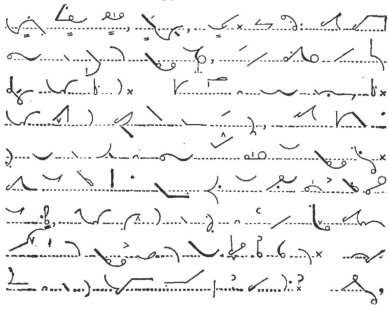

Exercise 51.

Write in Shorthand.

Spencer & Reed,
      New-York, N. Y.
Sirs:

Each season *in-the* past six *years we-have* bought *your* books *of* science *and-have-had to* pay excessive rates *on-*same. We emphasize *this* fact *because if-we-are to-*make *a* success *of-our* business *we-must* sell *the* books *at* low rates. Can you suggest how *we-may* get-*the* charges reduced, *or can you in-any-way* assist *us in* reducing-*the* cost *of-the* books?

                              Yours-respectfully,

Exercise 52.

Write in Shorthand.

Massey & Doyle,
      Worcester, Mass.
Sirs:

We-have-yours of-the 20th, *and you-may-*rely *on our* mailing *you-the* policy *on-*Saturday *next. We-have-seen-the* assessor *to-*day *and-have* induced *him to-*sign-*the* necessary forms. *We-are-*sorry *to-have-had* such *a* delay *in-this-*case, *but-we-have-had to-*move cautiously *so-as-to* insure success.

                              Yours-respectfully,

LESSON 11.

REVIEW.

57. The following is a brief review of the rules given in the last four lessons:

(a) The circle *s* is written *backward* to a *straight letter*, *inside* a *curve*, and *outside* of an *angle*.

(b) The loops *st* and *str*, and the circles *sw* and *ss* follow the *same rule of writing* as the *circle s*.

(c) A circle or loop is always read *first* at the *beginning* of a word, and *last* at the *end*.

(d) A *stroke* consonant must be written when a *word begins* or *ends* with a *sounded vowel*.

(e) The stroke ⌒ is written in the *same direction* as the *circle and curve* which it precedes or follows.

(f) The word *the* may be joined to a preceding word by means of a light tick.

(g) The *sw* circle is used in phrasing to express the words *as we;* and the *ss* circle is used to express the two *s*'s in such phrases as ⟶ in this city.

(h) Upward R is written in words like ⟶ *roar*, ⟶ *aware*, ⟶ *sincere*, in order to avoid an awkward outline.

(i) The *stroke s* is the *first* sign to be written in words *commencing with s-vowel-s*, and it is the *last* sign to be written in words *ending with* a diphthong followed by *-ous;* as ⟶ *saucer*, ⟶ *joyous*.

(j) The *initial* or *final vowel* may be *indicated by the outline* in such words as ⟶ *argue*, ⟶ *arrive*,

50 COURSE IN ISAAC PITMAN SHORTHAND.

acid, misty, jury, salary.

(k) An *unaccented short vowel* in the middle of a word may usually be *omitted*.

Exercise 53.

Read, copy, and transcribe.

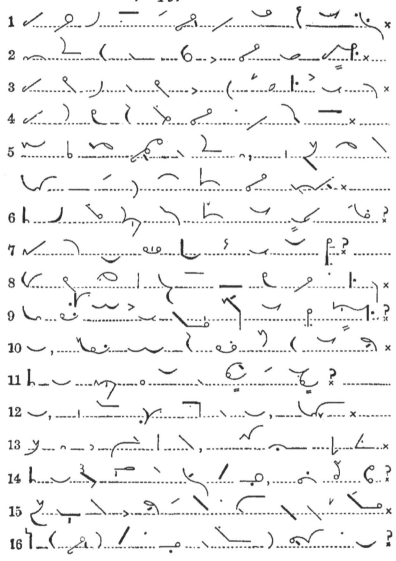

REVIEW.

Exercise 54.

Write in Shorthand.

1. *It ought-to be our wish to-do all-we-can to* assist *them.*
2. *Oh! yes, they-may all come to see us, if-they wish.*
3. *I-shall* ask *him to-speak to-them, and give them a special* lesson *when-they come.*
4. *Those-who know-the* best, say *it-is an* easy *language.*
5. *I-myself have a much different* view; *and-I-must own it-was beyond-me to*-master *it.*
6. *I-shall-be happy to see each youth* take *a different* lesson, *and-we-shall-see which* does-*the* best.
7. *We-had almost to* force *him to* use *his influence in-the--case, and-I-*fear *it-is of no* use now.
8. *I-must* ask-*them to-go to-the* city *themselves and see to-it.*
9. *Can-we-do nothing to* assist *the youth?*
10. *I-shall-be happy to-do anything you think* best.
11. *I-must-*say *I-think-we ought to-do-something.*
12. *I-*am-sorry *to* say *you-may-as-*well *give it up.*
13. *If-his* cousin *is to-come* also, *as-is* supposed, *I-shall-be--most happy.*
14. *We-are-*sorry *to know you-are to-*leave *New York.*
15. *We-shall-have to-go ourselves and see-the thing.*
16. *What-do-you think-they-*will-*do when-they see we-had to-*take *a special* car?
17. *I-think-they-*will stay away, *because of-the* cost.
18. *Do-you know-the* name *of-the* vessel *in-the* dock?

LESSON 12.

INITIAL HOOKS TO STRAIGHT STROKES.

58. A small initial hook, written in the *opposite* direction to that taken by the hands of a clock, adds *l* to the straight consonants ＼＼ │ │ ／／ — — thus forming a series of *double* consonants; as

    pl *bl* *tl* *dl* *ch l* *jl* *kl* *gl*

59. A small initial hook, written in the *same* direction as that taken by the hands of a clock, adds *r* to the same consonants, thus

    pr *br* *tr* *dr* *ch r* *jr* *kr* *gr*

60. These double consonants are named *pel* (as in *people*), *per* (as in *taper*), etc., to distinguish them from outlines formed by the separate letters, as (*pee-el*), (*pee-ar*). Vowels are placed and read to these double consonants just as they are to single consonants; thus *cup*, *couple*, *coupler*, *apply*, *press*, *impress*, *impressing*.

Exercise 55.

Read, copy, and transcribe.

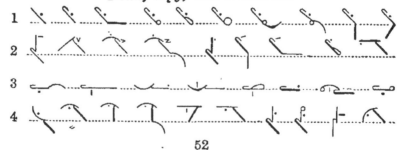

INITIAL HOOKS.

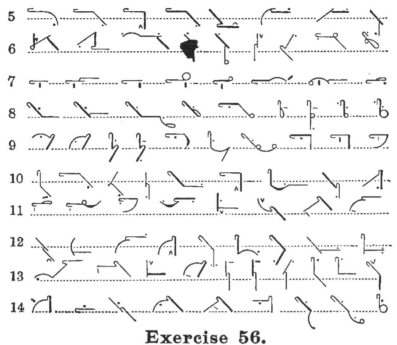

Exercise 56.

GRAMMALOGUES.

apply, people, by all, able, belief or believe-d, at all, tell, till, deliver-ed-y.

Write in Shorthand.

1. *If-you*-will `apply` to Major Gray *he-may-be-able to--tell-you.*
2. *It-is believed the* Major *may-be* away *till-the first of--*April.
3. We hope *to be-able to-deliver-the* cases *to*-morrow.
4. *We-do our* best *at-all* costs *to-*make delivery *when* promised.
5. *Have-you delivered-the* blue *and* black cloth *to* Briggs *and* Baker?
6. *Tell-the* auditor *to-take-the* ledger *and see what* Peters owes.
7. *What-is-the* least price *at-which-you-can* deliver *your* brass paste *in* glass bottles?

54 COURSE IN ISAAC PITMAN SHORTHAND.

8. *We-are* mailing *you* samples *of* cream lace *to*-day, *and-we*-regret *we-were*-unable *to-do-so till* now. *We--believe you-can-do no* better *at-the*-prices.

GRAMMALOGS AND PHRASEOGRAMS.

dollar-s,   call,   equal-ly,   doctor,   dear,   during,   Dear Sir,   Yours truly.

Exercise 57.
Read, copy, and transcribe.

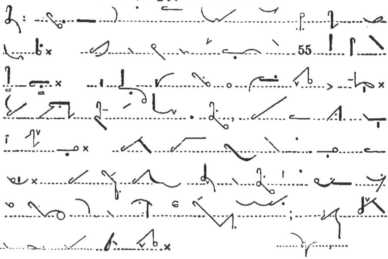

Exercise 58.
Write in Shorthand.

Samuel Brooks,
     Troy, *N. Y.*

Dear-Sir:

May I bring *to-your* notice *the* enclosed price-list *and* samples *of-the* fabrics *you saw during your call* last Wednesday? *I*-am-*able to-deliver these in* blue, black, or gray, *in a* couple *of*-days. The fabrics *are all equally* durable, *and-they-have no equals at-the*-prices. *I* also enclose *a* notice *of-my usual* April sale, *and shall-be--pleased to-have-you call and* look *at-my* stock.

                  Yours-truly,

LESSON 13.

INITIAL HOOKS TO CURVES.

61. A *large* initial hook adds *l* to any curved consonant *except* ⌒ *l,* ⌒ *r,*) *s,*) *z,*) *zh,* ⌣ *ng;* thus

    ℂ   ℂ   ((   )   ⌒   ⌣
    fl   *vl*   *th l*   *th l*   *sh l*   *ml*   *nl*

62. A *small* initial hook adds *r* to any curved consonant *except* ⌒ *l,* ⌒ *r,*) *s,*) *z;* thus

    ℂ   ℂ   ((   )   )   ⌒   ⌣
    fr   *vr*   *th r*   *th r*   *sh r*   *zh r*   *mr*   *nr*

63. The sound *ng-r*, as in ⌣ *singer*, ⌣ *wringer*, is comparatively rare; hence, the sign ⌣ is used to represent the more common sounds of *ng-kr* and *ng-gr* as heard in the words ⌣ *banker*, ⌣ *thinker*, ⌣ *finger*, ⌣ *linger*. The double consonant *sh l* is almost always written *upward*, as ⌣ *official;* while *sh r*) is GENERALLY written *downward*, as ⌣ *pressure*.

Exercise 59.
Read, copy, and transcribe.

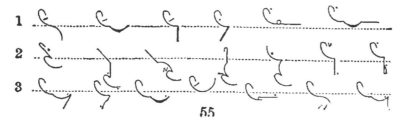

GRAMMALOGUES AND CONTRACTIONS.

 for, over, ever-y, valuation, evil,
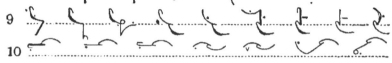 other, more or remark-ed, remarkable-y,
 mere or Mr., nor or in our, near,
 initial-ed-ly.

Exercise 60.

Write in Shorthand.

1. *The remarkable* affray *is over, and every* wise thinker *is* pleased.
2. *As Mr.* Frank Floyd *remarked, the* effects *of an evil* measure *may* last *for-ever.*
3. *We saw Mr.* Tinker, *the* banker, *in* Yonkers *on*-Friday last.
4. *He-was near-the* flower stall *in* Fourth Avenue; *but-we -have-*seen *nothing of-him* since, *nor-have-we-had any* business *in-the* bank.

INITIAL HOOKS TO CURVES. 57

5. *We-know no-more.*
6. *No, we-had no other* talk *with Mr.* Tinker, *beyond a mere remark on-the* state *of* business.
7. *The* banker *was remarkably* nervous, *it-is-*said, *but* brimful *of* energy, hopeful, *and* ready, *you would think, to* conquer *any* trouble *or* adversity.
8. *Oh, yes; he-was a* total abstainer, *and* drinkers were simply offensive *to-him.*

PHRASEOGRAMS.

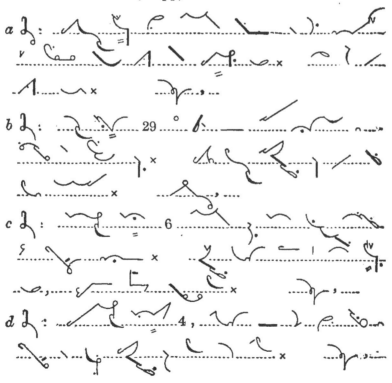

Exercise 61.
Read, copy, and transcribe.

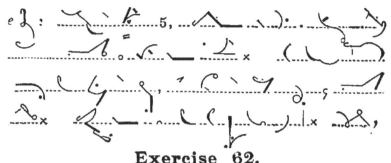

Exercise 62.
Write in Shorthand.

(a) *Dear*-Sir:

Your-favor *of-May* 4th *has* just *come to us, and-in*-reply *we*-beg *to* say *the* tank *you* sold *us* last April does *all-you* claim *and-more*. *We-think-it remarkably* cheap, *nor do we-think-it* likely *we-shall* use *any other.*

      Yours-truly,

(b) *Dear*-Sirs:

I-am-in-receipt-of-your-favor *of* July 27th, *and--in-reply* beg *to* enclose samples *of* Zephyrs *as near as I-can* get *to-your* shade. Trusting *these may* suit *you,*

      Yours-respectfully,

(c) *Dear*-Sir:

We-have-your-favor *of-the* 10th, *and* regret-*the* trouble caused *you by-the* error *of-our* entry clerk. Please charge *us with-the* overcharge *on-the* forty pieces.

      Respectfully-yours,

(d) Afraid, fraud, author, freed, differ, inner.
Owner, honor, banner, fisher, primer, aimer.
Bunker, anger, shrewd, shroud, shrank, shrub.
Flash, flavor, flax, flask, flap, flank.
Bushel, muffle, grapnel, approval, shrivel.
Flipper, reproval, hopeful, heedful, mindful.
Tanner, dinner, joiner, liner, fragile, freckles.
Driver, drover, shovel, thinner, vainer, froth.

LESSON 14.

INITIAL HOOKS TO CURVES (Concluded).

64. The curves ⟍ *r* and ⟩ *s*, not being hooked for *l* or *r* (see paragraphs 61 and 62), are hooked to provide extra forms for *fl* and *fr*, and *th l* and *th r* respectively, the signs thus obtained being thickened for the corresponding heavy consonants; as

⟍ ⟍ ⟍ ⟍   ⟩   ⟩   ⟩   ⟩
fl *vl* *fr* *vr* *th l* *th l* *th r* *th r*

The initial hook to ⌒ *l* is explained in a later lesson.

65. (*a*) The left curves for ⌒ ⌒ ⌒ ⌒ etc., are employed when they *stand alone* and are preceded by a vowel; as ⌒ *aflow*, ⌒ *evil*, ⌒ *offer*, ⌒ *author*.

(*b*) The right curves ⟍ ⟍ ⟩ etc., are employed when they stand alone and are *not* preceded by a vowel; as ⟍ *flow*, ⟩ *free*, ⟩ *throw*.

66. When joined to another stroke consonant, the form is used which gives the better joining. The following illustrations will serve as a guide to the students: ⟍ *flap*, ⟍ *flighty*, ⟍ *fledge*, ⟍ *fluffy*, ⟍ *floor*, ⟍ *flake*, ⟍ *flag*, ⟍ *flame*, ⟍ *arrival*, ⟍ *muffle*, ⟍ *rival*, ⟍ *inflame*, ⟍ *Fred*, ⟍ *average*, ⟍ *froth*, ⟍ *Jefferson*, ⟍ *verb*, ⟍ *freak*, ⟍ *throb*, ⟍ *Dover*, ⟍ *coffer*, ⟍ *laugher*

Exercise 63.

Read, copy, and transcribe.

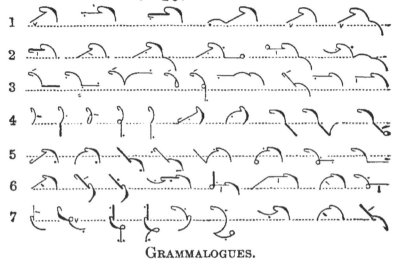

GRAMMALOGUES.

from, very, however, they are, their, there, through, therefore, principle, principal-ly, liberty, member or remembered, number-ed.

Exercise 64.

Write in Shorthand.

1. *It-was, however, through their principal member the* firm *was able to* secure *the* business *in* leather.
2. *They-are* likely *to-*succeed.
3. *It-is very* true, *but it-*seems almost incredible *there--should-be* such *a large-number of-members in-the* club.
4. *I-shall-be at* liberty *to-*morrow *from* five o'clock *to* six, *and-I-shall, therefore, be-*pleased *to see-you if-you-can* give me a call *at-my* house.
5. *I-remember-the* cases, *and-they-*were numbered 25 to 40.
6. *I-have-*seen-*the* packer, too, and he remembered-*the* numbers easily.
7. He agrees *with* me, *and you-may, therefore,* take-*the* numbers *as* right.
8. *They-are very* easily remembered.

INITIAL HOOKS TO CURVES.

PHRASEOGRAMS.

Very truly yours, early reply, your reply, I am very sorry, I shall be pleased.

Exercise 65.

Read, copy, and transcribe.

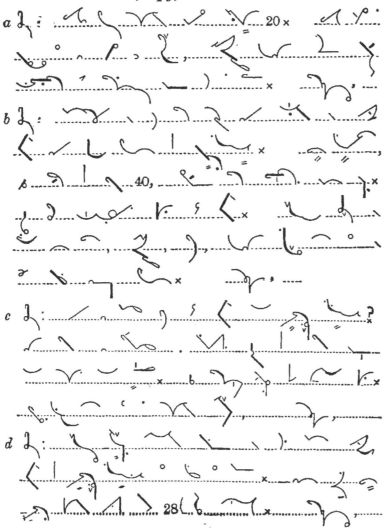

Exercise 66.

Write in Shorthand.

1. Novel, snivel, hovel, ruffles, influx, snowflake.
2. Phrase, phrases, phrased, paraphrase, freeze.
3. Thrice, thrusts, tethers, gathers, throngs, wafer.
4. Bather, bother, Arthur, clever, cleverly, cleverness.
5. Reefer, briefer, belfry, craver, rover, Bethel.
6. Lethal, breather, recover, cleaver, clover.
7. *Go* right *through-the principal* avenue, *and you*-will--see *Mr.* Parker's *house by-the* side *of-the* river.
8. Follow *the principles of-liberty through* life, *and you*-will-*be a* true citizen *and a* worthy *member of* society.
9. Look *your* trouble bravely *in-the* face, *and you*-will *very*-likely discover *a way to* conquer *it, however* severe *it-may-seem at-the first*.
10. *Remember,* he *who* wavers *in-his* resolve *is already* half lost. *Your* aim *is to*-succeed *in-your* lessons. *Therefore, be very* firm, *and go through-the* exercises set *for-you as*-well-*as you-can. They-are specially* devised *for-you.*
11. *Do-you remember-the number of Mr.* Frederick's room *at-the* Waverley Hotel?
12. *I-know-the* price *was* $5.
13. *The* frivolous clerk *was much* flurried *on-the* arrival *of-his* employer. *He should remember there-is a* time *for everything, and-it-is* wrong *to* trifle *during* business *hours.*

LESSON 15.

CIRCLES AND LOOPS PREFIXED TO INITIAL HOOKS.

67. The circle *s* is prefixed to hooked curves and to straight consonants hooked for *l*, by writing the circle *inside the hook;* thus ⌇ *cipher,* ⌇ *decipher* ⌇ *sever,* ⌇ *dissever,* ⌇ *signer,* ⌇ *designer,* ⌇ *civil,* ⌇ *peaceful,* ⌇ *sable,* ⌇ *disable,* ⌇ *settle,* ⌇ *pedestal,* ⌇ *sickle,* ⌇ *bicycle.*

68. The circles *s* and *sw* and the loop *st* are prefixed to straight consonants hooked for *r*, by writing the circle or loop on the *same side as the hook*, so that the circle or loop may be supposed to include the hook; thus ⌇ *upper,* ⌇ *supper,* ⌇ *sweeper,* ⌇ *steeper,* ⌇ *prosper,* ⌇ *eater,* ⌇ *sitter,* ⌇ *sweeter,* ⌇ *stouter,* ⌇ *destroy,* ⌇ *ochre,* ⌇ *soaker,* ⌇ *stoker,* ⌇ *swagger,* ⌇ *jack-screw.*

69. When a circle and hook occur medially *at an angle*, both circle and hook *must be shown;* thus ⌇ *pastry,* ⌇ *clasper,* ⌇ *extra,* ⌇ *mistrust,* ⌇ *lustrous,* ⌇ *reciter,* ⌇ *listener.* When ⌇ or ⌇ follows *t* or *d*, it is written thus: ⌇ *Tasker,* ⌇ *tusker,* ⌇ *disgrace.*

Exercise 67.
Read, copy, and transcribe.

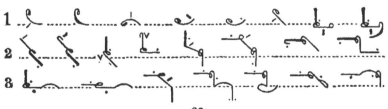

COURSE IN ISAAC PITMAN SHORTHAND.

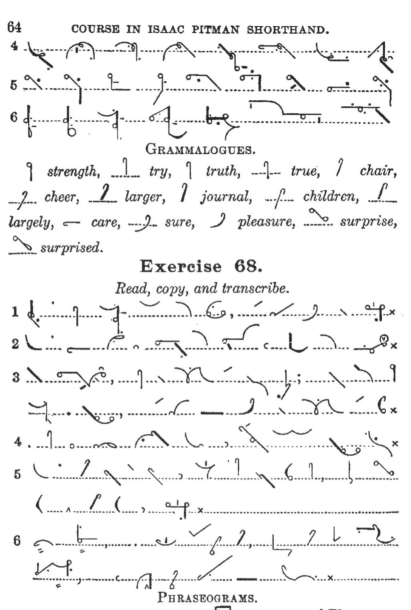

GRAMMALOGUES.

strength, try, truth, true, chair, cheer, larger, journal, children, largely, care, sure, pleasure, surprise, surprised.

Exercise 68.

Read, copy, and transcribe.

PHRASEOGRAMS.

I can assure you, I regret, I am surprised.

Exercise 69.

Write in Shorthand.

Dear-Sir: In-reply-to-your-favor of-the 14th, your cycles shall-be-delivered as early next month as I-can

CIRCLES AND LOOPS. 65

possibly get *them out*. *I*-regret *I*-am-unable *to-deliver* sooner, *and I-can*-assure-*you it-would-be a pleasure to* oblige-*you if*-possible. *I*-am-*surprised to know you have* still *to see-the* new saddles, *and-I*-am mailing *you half a* dozen samples *to*-day. *Yours-respectfully*,

Exercise 70.
Read, copy, and transcribe.

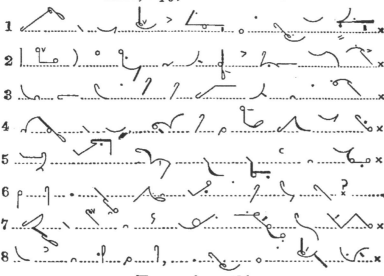

Exercise 71.
Write in Shorthand.

1. Noticeable, stater, stager, stitcher, stutter.
2. Passable, classical, blissful, displace, rasper.
3. Deceiver, expresses, satchel, suckle, supplies.
4. Safer, sever, sufferance, upspring, supersede.
5. Scribe, suitor, streak, spruce, straw, strays.
6. Sadder, supreme, string, scraper, strainer.
7. *We-are*-sorry *to-have to* destroy *the* claim.
8. *I*-am-*surprised you-should* suppress *it*.
9. *I-can*-assure-*you I-have* seldom seen *him*.
10. *I*-regret *to see so* strong *a* case *on-the other*-side.
11. *It-may-be a* struggle, *but-we-shall* scramble *through*.
12. *I*-am-*sure you would-do nothing* dishonorable.

5 S. C.

LESSON 16.

N AND F HOOKS.

70. A small final hook, written in the *same* direction as that taken by the hands of a clock, adds *n* to any straight consonant; thus ⟍ *pain*, ⊥ *tone*, ⟋ *chain*, ⟍ *coin*, ⟋ *run*, ⟋ *won*, ⌒ *hen*.

71. A small final hook, written in the *opposite* direction to that taken by the hands of a clock, adds *f* or *v* to any straight consonant; thus ⟍ *pave*, ⊥ *tough*, ⌐ *chafe*, ⌒ *cough*, ⟋ *rough*, ⟋ *wove*, ⟋ *heave*.

72. A small final hook, written *inside* the curve, adds *n* to any curved consonant; thus ⟋ *fain*, ⟋ *oven*, ⟋ *thin*, ⟋ *thine*, ⟋ *assign*, ⟋ *zone*, ⟋ *ocean*, ⟋ *mine*, ⟋ *known*, ⟋ *loan*, ⟋ *earn*.

73. The *n* and *f* hooks may be employed medially when they join easily with the following stroke; thus ⟋ *punish*, ⟋ *training*, ⟋ *coining*, ⟋ *runner*, ⟋ *paving*, ⟋ *deafness*, ⟋ *chafing*, ⟋ *refer*.

74. A hook at the end of a word is always read *last;* so that when a word ends with a *sounded vowel*, a stroke consonant must be written; thus ⟋ *pony*, ⟋ *deny*, ⟋ *honey*, ⟋ *puffy*, ⟋ *coffee*, ⟋ *funny*, ⟋ *shiny*, ⟋ *money*. The student should refer again to paragraph 55, when he will see that what is there said with regard to *vowel indication* applies to the present paragraph also.

75. Final *r*, when hooked, is generally written *upward*, as ⟋ *born*, ⟋ *turn*, ⟋ *adjourn*, ⟋ *corn*, ⟋ *turf*, ⟋ *scarf*.

"N" AND "F" HOOKS.   67

Exercise 72.
Read, copy, and transcribe.

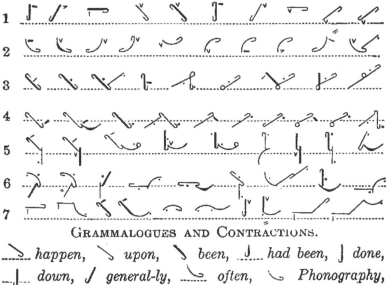

GRAMMALOGUES AND CONTRACTIONS.

⟍ happen, ⟍ upon, ⟍ been, ⌡ had been, ⌡ done, ⌡ down, ∕ general-ly, ⟋ often, ⟍ Phonography, ⟍ phonographer, ⟍ phonographic, ⟍ have been, ⟨ within, ⟨ southern, ⎯ northern.

Exercise 73.
Read, copy, and transcribe.

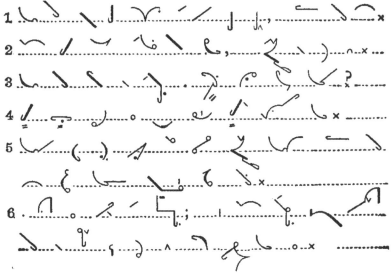

68 COURSE IN ISAAC PITMAN SHORTHAND

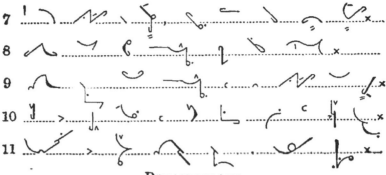

PHRASEOGRAMS.

referring to your favor, *referring to yours*, *enclose-d herewith*, *best class*.

Exercise 74.
Write in Shorthand.

(a) Mr. David Green, Lincoln Hotel, Brooklyn, N. Y.

Dear-Sir: Referring-*to*-*yours* *of*-*the* 24th June, *we*--*are*-pleased *with*-*the* proof *of*-*your* activity, *and*-trust *your* Brooklyn visit *may* turn *out* even *more* profitable than *you* imagine. *We*-*are* mailing *you* *to*-day *the* sample *of* linen napkin *for*-*which*-*you* ask. *We*-enclose-herewith *a* small length *of* fancy satin ribbon, *which*-*you*-will-please add *to*--*your*-*other* samples. *We should* like *you* *to*-make *a* special call upon Thornley & Craven. *We*-*have*-*done* nothing *with*--*them* since *you* were *down there* last-*year*, *and*-*we* *happen to* know their general business *is remarkably* brisk just-now.

Yours-*truly*,

(b) *Mr.* Henry Canning, Orange, N. J.

Dear-Sir: *We*-*have*-*your*-favor *of*-*the* 11th, *and*-*in*--reply *we*-*have*-*the*-*pleasure* *to* enclose-herewith price-list *of*-*our* new "Milton Flyer" sewing machine, *a* machine *which*-*is* far *in* advance *of any* make *we*-*have*-*ever* sold. *The* cheap machine *to*-*which*-*you*-refer *is a* foreign one, *which*--*we* decline *to*-keep *in* stock. *We* prefer *to* offer *nothing but*-*the* best-class. Our local agent *is very often near your*--place, *and*-*we*-*shall* ask *him* *to*-*call*-*upon you* *and* explain *more* fully *all*-*we* claim *for*-*the* " Milton Flyer."

Respectfully-*yours*,

"N" AND "F" HOOKS.

Exercise 75.
Read, copy, and transcribe.

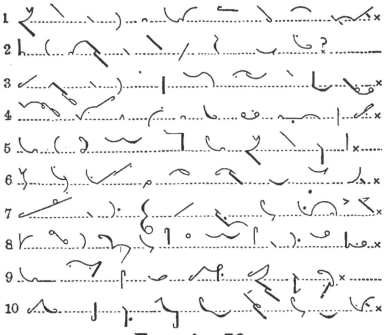

Exercise 76.
Write in Shorthand.

1. Wooden, maintain, bacon, taken, spoken, restrain.
2. Abandon, banish, opening, winner, millinery.
3. Cuff, buff, dove, chief, rave, calf, serf.
4. Striving, driving, provoke, defeat, davit.
5. Balloon, Japan, flown, kitchen, coffin, disdain.
6. Syphon, saloon, none, spurn, marine, churn.
7. *If-you*-labor *beyond-your strength you*-will-*have to see-the doctor.*
8. Ask *your* cousin Fanny *to* favor *us with a* song.
9. *I*-am-*sure you*-will like *Phonography* when *you* begin *to*-learn *it*.
10. *Would you care to*-take-*the-chair at-the* gathering?
11. *I-think-the* General *was within his* rights.
12. *We often go down to* see *Dr.* Sutton *at-the* beach.

LESSON 17.

CIRCLES AND LOOPS ADDED TO FINAL HOOKS.

76. A circle or loop is added to the hook *n* attached to *straight* consonants, by writing the circle or loop on the *same side* as the hook; thus ⌡ Dan, ⌡ dance, ⌡ dances, ⌡ danced, ⌡ Dunster.

77. A *medial* circle represents *s only;* so that when *ns* occurs in the middle of a word, both letters *must be shown;* thus ⌡ dancer, ⌡ Spencer, ⌡ ransom, ⌡ winsome, ⌡ pencil, ⌡ density, ⌡ cancer, ⌡ fencer, ⌡ rancid, ⌡ ransack.

78. The circle *s* is added to the hook *f*, and to the hook *n* when attached to *curved consonants*, by writing the circle *inside the hook;* thus ⌡ paves, ⌡ doves, ⌡ cliffs, ⌡ serves, ⌡ fines, ⌡ frowns, ⌡ moans, ⌡ loans.

79. The sign ⌡ *ns* is used to represent the *light* sound of *ns* after a *curved* consonant; thus ⌡ Vance, ⌡ romance. The effect of this rule is that the outlines for related words of this class are kept regular in construction; thus ⌡ mince, ⌡ minces, ⌡ minced, ⌡ mincing, ⌡ fence, ⌡ fences, ⌡ fenced, ⌡ fencing, ⌡ lance, ⌡ lances, ⌡ lanced.

CIRCLES AND LOOPS.

Exercise 77.
Read, copy, and transcribe.

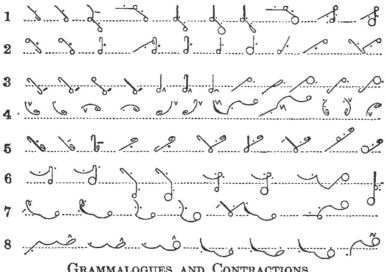

GRAMMALOGUES AND CONTRACTIONS.

approve, behalf, above, out of, advantage, difficult, difficulty, which have, suggestion, suggestive, one, opinion, altogether, together, insurance

Exercise 78.
Read, copy, and transcribe.

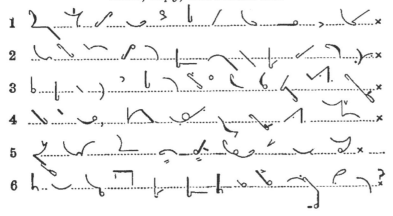

COURSE IN ISAAC PITMAN SHORTHAND.

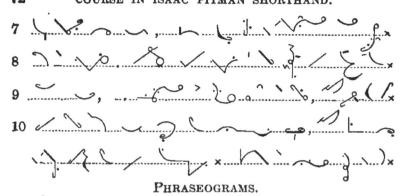

PHRASEOGRAMS.

at once,   *first class,*   *for the first time,*
from first to last,   *in the first place.*

Exercise 79.

Write in Shorthand.

(a) Mr. Graves has, *from-first-to*-last, *given* preference *to-the* new scheme *of insurance for* private residences. *It-is a first-*class office, *and, if-you approve, he*-says *it-would-be an advantage for-you to*-take--*out* a policy now. *There-is-nothing difficult to* arrange, *and you*-will-*have-no-difficulty in* obtaining references, *should you* desire *them.*

(b) *It-is, above all,* necessary *to*-exercise vigilance *in-the* avoidance *of* risk *in-this insurance* business, *and--with all* deference *to Mr.* Graves, *I* disagree *with--his opinion. In-the-first-*place, *he-is* wrong *in* placing *all-his* risks *in-one* office; *and,* then, *for--the-first-*time *during-the* years *I-have*-known *him, he-has, in-this-*instance, dispensed *with-the care he usually* displays. *I-think he-is altogether* wrong.

(c) *It* remains *to be*-seen *how-the* lancer behaves *with-the* reserves. *If-he* swerves *from-the* right, *he-will--have to put up with-the* rebuffs *of-his* fellows. He deserves success, *and-if-he* observes *what I-have* advised *him, and* proves *his* bravery, *he*-will soon win *it.*

(d) *The* substance *of-the* charge against *the youth was* gone into, *and-it-was* shown *he-was* merely guilty *of* imprudence. *Up to-the* spring, *he had* borne *a first-*class name. *We*-were *together at-the* review.

CIRCLES AND LOOPS.

Exercise 80.
Read, copy, and transcribe.

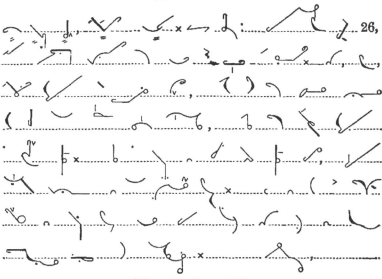

Exercise 81.
Write in Shorthand.

1. Bounce, bounced, bounces, trounce, trounced, trounces.
2. Bronze, bronzed, bronzes, prance, pranced, prances.
3. Hence, clowns, cleansed, cleanses, distance, distances.
4. Alliance, flounce, flounced, flounces, affianced, silenced.
5. Cleaves, grooves, starves, motives, sheriffs, tariffs.
6. Thrones, zones, lens, refrains, shuns, veins, nouns.
7. *Mr.* James Burns,
        Dover, Del.
  Dear-Sir:
    We ask *your* acceptance *and* perusal *of-the* enclosed price-list *of first*-class wines *from* American grapes, *which-we-are*-now ready *to* offer *our* patrons at-prices far below *those usually* paid *for* foreign wines. *Our* customers *have our* assurance *as-to-the* purity, flavor, *and general* excellence *of-these* wines, *and-they-may* place *the* utmost reliance *on our* guarantee. *It-has-been our* aim *from-first-to*-last, *to*-maintain *a* name *for* wines *of-the* finest flavor, *and-we-believe we-have-done this*. *May-we* deliver*-you* a sample case?
                    Yours-respectfully

LESSON 18.

REVIEW.

80. The last six lessons may be summarized as follows:

(a) The hooks *l* and *f*, when attached to *straight* letters, are written in the *opposite direction* to that taken by the hands of a clock; as ⟨⟩ *bluff*, ⟨⟩ *cliff*.

(b) The hooks *r* and *n*, when attached to *straight* letters, are written in the *same direction* as that taken by the hands of a clock; as ⟨⟩ *brain*, ⟨⟩ *crown*.

(c) The hook *l*, when attached to a *curved consonant*, is a large initial hook; as ⟨⟩ *fled*.

(d) The hooks *r* and *n*, when attached to a *curved consonant*, are *small hooks*; as ⟨⟩ *frown*, ⟨⟩ *shrine*.

(e) The sign ⟨⟩ represents the sounds *ng-kr*, or *ng-gr*; as ⟨⟩ *banker*, ⟨⟩ *finger*.

(f) When standing alone, the left curves ⟨⟩ ⟨⟩ ⟨⟩ ⟨⟩ ⟨⟩ ⟨⟩ are used *if a vowel precedes*, and the right curves ⟨⟩ ⟨⟩ ⟨⟩ ⟨⟩ if a vowel does *not* precede; as ⟨⟩ *offer*, ⟨⟩ *author*, ⟨⟩ *aflow*, ⟨⟩ *fray*, ⟨⟩ *throw*, ⟨⟩ *flow*.

(g) As a rule, the *right curves* ⟨⟩ ⟨⟩ etc., are joined to strokes written *towards the right*, while the *left curves* ⟨⟩ ⟨⟩ etc., are joined to strokes written *towards the left*; as ⟨⟩ *wafer*, ⟨⟩ *waver*, ⟨⟩ *Jeffrey*, ⟨⟩ *average*.

REVIEW.

(*h*) The circle *s* is prefixed or affixed to *hooked curves* and to *straight letters* hooked for *l* or *f*, by writing the circle *inside the hook;* thus ⟋ *suffer*, ⟋ *moans*, ⟋ *supply*, ⟋ *griefs*.

(*i*) A circle or loop is prefixed or affixed to a straight letter hooked for *r* or *n*, by writing the circle or loop on the *same side as the hook;* thus ⟋ *strains*, ⟋ *stoker*, ⟋ *dance*, ⟋ *dances*.

(*j*) A final hook, like a final circle or loop, is always *read last;* thus ⟋ *brawn*, but ⟋ *brawny;* ⟋ *brave*, but ⟋ *bravo*.

Exercise 82.

Read, copy, and transcribe.

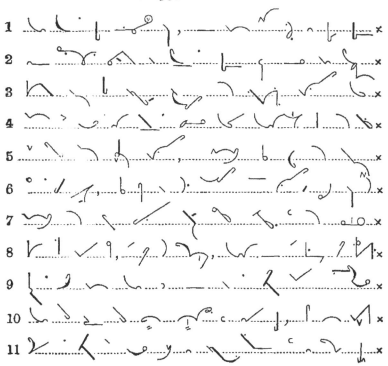

12
13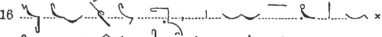
14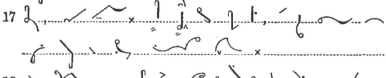
15
16
17
18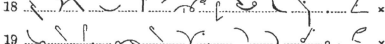
19

Exercise 83.

Write in Shorthand.

1. *Shall you be in New York this year or next ?*
2. *Has your young* brother *done anything with-the* French *language ?*
3. *How-much is owing on-the things you* bought *from* Cliffs ?
4. *Do-you know anything at-all of-the remarkable Mr.* Vance ?
5. *Do-you think Mr.* France *can be influenced in-his--favor ?*
6. *I-am* almost *sure your Mr.* Bright *is a mere* fraud.
7. *I-think-it-is most-*likely *I-shall-be down on-the first of* June.
8. *Our* picnic takes-place *as usual on-the first of next* month.
9. *Do-you think-you-are* likely *to-come ?*
10. *I-shall* call *and* see-you *myself when-the* time *comes* near.

11. *Oh*, *yes*, *we-shall* provide *the* music *ourselves*, *as-is* *usual*.

12. *I-saw-the* truck *at-the* door *half an hour ago*.

13. *We-have-your-*favor *of* August 10th, *and-we-thank-you for-your* early-reply.

14. *Dear-*Sir:

　　Please favor *us with a* copy *of-your-*latest list *of* books suitable *for* prizes, *and-*oblige.
　　　　　　　　　　　　　　Yours-truly,

15. *Dear-*Sir:

　　*I-am-in-*receipt-*of-your-*favor *of-*Wednesday, *and--in-*reply beg *to* enclose-herewith copy *of-our* list *of* new books.
　　　　　　　　　　　　Respectfully-yours,

16. *Dear-*Sirs:

　　*In-*reply-*to-your-*favor *of-*March 30th, *I-*regret *very-much the* delay *in-the* delivery *of-your* candies *and--*preserves. *I-have-had a* breakdown *in-the* machinery, *and* hence *the* delay. *I-*trust *you-*will-favor *me with your* indulgence *for a* few-days *more*.
　　　　　　　　　　　　Yours-respectfully,

17. *Dear-*Sir:

　　I-have-yours of-the 16th, *and-I-shall-see to-the* dispatch *of-the* books *in-*time *for-your* purpose. *I-am--*pleased *to know you have-had a* busy season.
　　　　　　　　　　　　　　Yours-truly,

LESSON 19.

SHUN HOOK.

81. A *large* final hook expresses the light or heavy sound of *-tion* (shun), however spelled. The *shun* hook is written:

(*a*) *Inside* curves; thus ⌒ *fashion*, ⌒ *invasion*, ⌒ *nation*.

(*b*) On the *right* side of simple (that is not hooked or circled) *t, d,* or *j;* thus ⌒ *rotation*, ⌐ *dictation*, ⌐ *addition*, ⌐ *logician*.

(*c*) On the side *opposite to the last vowel* when added to a simple straight stroke *other than t, d,* or *j;* thus ⌐ *diction*, ⌐ *education*, ⌐ *passion*, ⌒ *option*, ⌐ *occasion*, ⌐ *action*.

(*d*) On the side *opposite to the hook or circle,* when added to a hooked or circled straight stroke; thus ⌒ *oppression*, ⌐ *attrition*, ⌐ *depletion*, ⌐ *deception*, ⌐ *suction*, ⌐ *discussion*.

(*e*) *Away from the curve,* when added to *k* or *g* springing from the curves *f, v,* or *upward l;* thus ⌐ *fiction*, ⌐ *navigation*, ⌒ *location*, ⌒ *selection*. The circle *s* is added thus: ⌒ *portions*, ⌒ *operations*.

Exercise 84.

Read, copy, and transcribe.

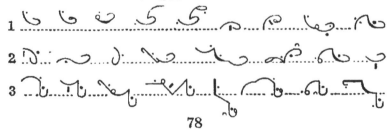

SHUN HOOK. 79

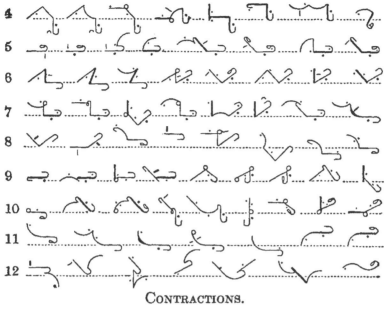

CONTRACTIONS.

architect-ure-al, neglect-ed, prospect, object-ed, subject-ed, expect-ed, unexpected-ly, respect-ed, suspect-ed, inspect-ed-ion.

Exercise 85.

Read, copy, and transcribe.

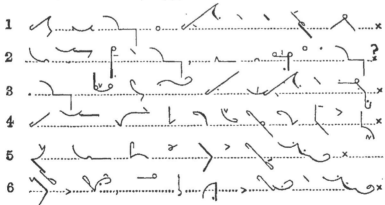

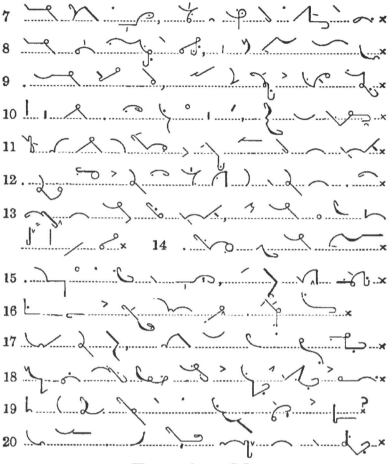

Exercise 86.

Write in Shorthand.

1. *If-you suspect-the truth of-the architect's* assertion, *go and see-the* erection.
2. *If-you neglect to object to-the* trespass, *you-will-have difficulty with-the* prosecution.
3. *You-should call unexpectedly and see them.*
4. *Is there any prospect of-the subject* being taken *for* discussion *in-the next* session?
5. *Does-the principal expect-the* infection *to* spread?
6. *By whose* authority *was-the* auction carried *on?*

7. *This-is-the first* intimation *I-have-had of-the* affair.
8. *You-*will-*have to put* off-*the* recitations *till-the inspection is over.*
9. *If-you have-no respect for-the-*man *you had* better take exception *to-his* inclusion.
10. *The* degradation *was unexpected, and-I-think-you--should* offer some reparation *for-your* implication.
11. Now *is-the* time *to* prove your affection *for-the neglected architect.*
12. *The* subject *has a* strange fascination *for a* man *of* resolution *who-has* also *a* taste *for* invention.
13. Tension, retention, population, designation.
14. Citation, sections, aggression, visitation, station.
15. Avocations, invocation, afflictions, flotation.
16. Capitation, repetition, editions, rations.
17. Apparition, extractions, aspirations, visions.
18. Visionary, commissioner, divisional, educational.

Exercise 87.

Read, copy, and transcribe.

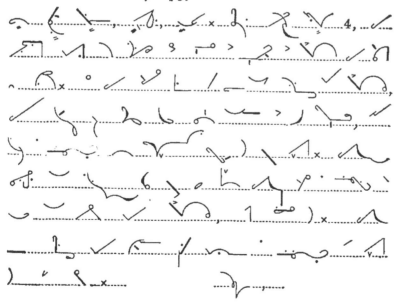

Exercise 88.

Write in Shorthand.

Mr. John Benson,
    Lancaster, Maine.
Dear-Sir·

We-are-in-receipt-*of-your*-favor *of* June 28th, *and*-*we* regret *it-is out-of-our* power *to*-make *any* reduction *in-the*-price *for-the* installation *of-the* gas engines. *We-have* gone *over-the* specifications again, *with-the* view *of* acceding *to-your wishes if*-possible, *but-the* inclusion *of a number of* severe restrictions *by-the architect* forces *us to-the* retention *of-the* price already *given. We-think on* reflection *you*-will-*see there-is every* reason *for our* prices, *and-we*-trust *to-receive-your* commission *to*-proceed *with-the* job.

Respectfully yours,

LESSON 20.

SHUN HOOK (Concluded).

82. The sound of *shun* is expressed after the circle *s* by a *small hook*, formed by continuing the circle on the *other side* of the stroke; thus ⟶ *position*, ⟶ *dispensation*. A third-place vowel between the circle and the *shun* hook is expressed by the vowel-sign being written outside the hook; thus ⟶ *physician*, ⟶ *transition*. When the hook is left unvocalized a second-place vowel is to be read between the circle and *shun;* thus ⟶ *possessions*, ⟶ *sensation*. First-place vowels do not occur between *s* and *shun*. The circle *s* may be added to the hook, as in the preceding examples.

83. When a diphthong and a vowel occur between *shun* and the preceding consonant, the stroke *sh* and the hook *n* are written, and *not* the *shun* hook; thus ⟶ *situation*, ⟶ *tuition*. This does not apply to such words as ⟶ *punctuation*, ⟶ *perpetuation*, where, in order to avoid an awkward outline, the large hook may be taken to represent *-uation*.

Exercise 89.
Read, copy, and transcribe.

COURSE IN ISAAC PITMAN SHORTHAND.

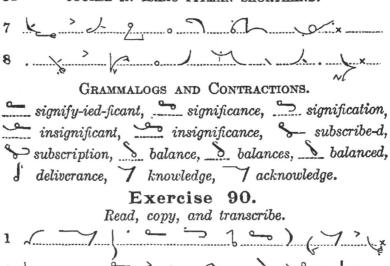

GRAMMALOGS AND CONTRACTIONS.

signify-ied-ficant, *significance*, *signification*, *insignificant*, *insignificance*, *subscribe-d*, *subscription*, *balance*, *balances*, *balanced*, *deliverance*, *knowledge*, *acknowledge*.

Exercise 90.
Read, copy, and transcribe.

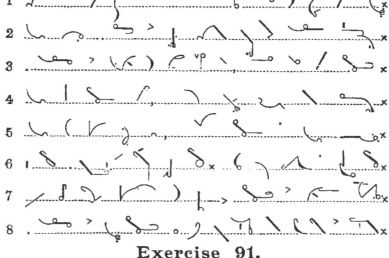

Exercise 91.
Write in Shorthand.

1. *If-you wish to subscribe*, please *signify the* same.
2. The fact *of-the* authorization being refused *was very significant.*
3. We hope *you see-the signification of-the insignificant* remark.
4. The *insignificance of-your subscription is* sure *to-raise* a commotion.
5. Please *acknowledge-the* receipt *of-the* book *on* taxation.

6. *Have-you any* knowledge *of-the* people *who* superscribe *the* register?
7. Some *of-the* superscriptions are scarcely legible.
8. *Are you in a* position *to subscribe to-the* society?
9. *Have-you-read-the* depositions, *and what-do-you think of-the* accusation?
10. *Your subscription may* cause vexation *and a* sensation.

PHRASEOGRAMS.

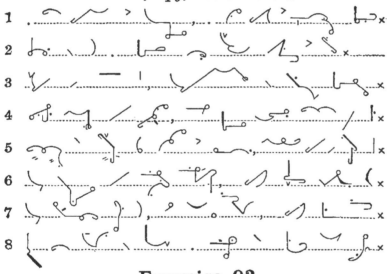

additional expense, additional cost, we are in a position, more and more, less and less, facts of the case.

Exercise 92.
Read, copy, and transcribe.

Exercise 93.
Write in Shorthand.

1. *What-do-you* know *of-the* facts-*of-the*-case?
2. *Are you* ready *to-go to* any additional-expense *in-the*-case?
3. *You-must-remember the* additional-cost *may-be* heavy.
4. *We-are-in-a*-position *to-*prove *the valuation was* unfair.

5. *We-have a very* strong suspicion *of-the* Prussian's motives.
6. *If-you-can tell us-the* date *of-the first* petition, *it-may* assist *us to* form *a* decision *on-the* facts-*of-the*-case.
7. *We*-suppose *there-was a* succession *of* petitions *at-the* instigation *of-the* Prussian.
8. *We-think, from-the* depositions, *the* man's *language is* actionable.
9. *We see no* extenuation *for-his* line *of* action.
10. *If-you call to-*morrow, *we-can* review *the* situation.

Exercise 94.
Write in Shorthand.

Mr. G. E. Goschen,
   Syracuse, *N. Y.*
*Dear-*Sir:

I-desire *to-call your* attention *to-the balance of* $9.04, due *by-you to-the* New Dictionary Agency *for* commission *over*paid. *You have* already *had a* thorough explanation *of-this balance from Mr*. Reeves, *and you-are, therefore, in* possession *of-the* facts-*of-the*-case. *I-can see no* reason *why you-should* refuse *to* settle-*the* claim, *and-I*-trust *to*-receive *a* remittance *by* return mail.

Yours-truly,

Mr. Harry Jones,
   Albany, *N. Y.*
*Dear-*Sir:

On-the 20th *of* August *you-*wrote *us to* say *we-had* invoiced ten gross escutcheons *at* $2.00 per gross, *in-*-place *of* $1.75, *which-you* said *was-the* price *given by-our* agent. *We-have-had our* salesman's price-list *in for* examination, *and-we see there-is-no-*such price *as* $1.75 *for--the-number-of* escutcheons *delivered to-you*. *In*-addition--*to-this, he-*says *he* sold none *at-all at-the-*price *you--*mention. *Your* supposition, *therefore, of an* error *in* invoicing *must-be* wrong, *and-we-must* decline *to* allow *you any* reduction.

Respectfully-yours,

LESSON 21.
COMPOUND CONSONANTS.

84. (a) A *large* initial hook adds *w* to *k* and *g;* thus ⌒ *quick,* ⌒ *Guam,* ⌒ *request,* ⌒ *sanguine.*

(b) A *small* initial hook adds *w* to upward *l*, while a *large* initial hook adds *wh* to the same letter; thus ⌒ *wile,* ⌒ *while,* ⌒ *wail,* ⌒ *whale,* ⌒ *weal,* ⌒ *wheel.*

(c) *Thickening* a *downward l* or *r*, adds *r* to these letters; thus ⌒ *fowler,* ⌒ *scaler,* ⌒ *sharer,* ⌒ *snorer.*

(d) *Thickening m* indicates the addition of *p* or *b;* thus ⌒ *pump,* ⌒ *bamboo,* ⌒ *empire,* ⌒ *embalm;* but when *l* or *r immediately* follows *mp* or *mb*, the simple ⌒ is written; thus ⌒ *employ,* ⌒ *impress,* ⌒ *emblem,* ⌒ *embrace.*

(e) *Enlarging* the initial hook of *w*, indicates the addition of the aspirate *h;* thus ⌒ *whistle,* ⌒ *whisk,* ⌒ *whip,* ⌒ *whirl.*

(f) The compound consonant ⌒ may be hooked for *r;* thus ⌒ *scamper,* ⌒ *slumber,* ⌒ *clamber.*

85. The initial hook in *wl* and *whl* is read *first;* so that if a vowel *precedes w*, the stroke must be written, and not the hook; as ⌒ *awhile.*

86. The compound consonants ⌒ *ler,* ⌒ *rer*, must *not* be employed when a vowel follows the *r;* so that the separate consonants are written in such words as ⌒ *raillery,* ⌒ *foolery,* ⌒ *aurora,* etc.

87. The remaining compound consonants of this series are vocalized like the single consonants, as in the examples given above.

88 COURSE IN ISAAC PITMAN SHORTHAND.

Letter.	Character.	Name.	As in
KW	⊂	kwā	*qu*ick, re*qu*est
GW	⊂	gwā	*gu*ava, lin*gu*al
WL	((up)	wel	*wail*, un*well*
WHL	((up)	hwel	*whale*, *whel*p
LR	((down)	ler	fee*ler*, nai*ler*
RR	) (down)	rer	poo*rer*, sha*rer*
MP, MB	⌒	{ emp / emb }	ca*mp*, e*mb*alm
WH	⌣	hwā	*wh*ere, *wh*isk

Exercise 95.
Read, copy, and transcribe.

COMPOUND CONSONANTS.

[shorthand exercises 12–15]

GRAMMALOGUES AND CONTRACTIONS.

will, *while*, *important-ce*, *improve-d-ment*, *impossible*, *improves-ments*, *whether*, *unquestionable-y*, *yesterday*, *January*, *February*, *November*, *United States*.

Exercise 96.

Read, copy, and transcribe.

[shorthand exercises 1–8]

Exercise 97.

Write in Shorthand.

1. *It-will-be impossible* to arrange such *important improvements for-the first* Monday *in February*.
2. You *see how important it-is for-you* to see *Mr*. Wheeler.

3. *I-fear-the importance of-the improvement will-be* lost sight *of in-the* hurry *of-the January* business.
4. *January will-be too near* Christmas; *we-must, unquestionably, have-the things done by November at-the* latest.
5. Please write *me whether you* prefer *to-come in January or in February.*
6. *While you-are-in* Boston, *it-will-be an unquestionable advantage for-you to-call on Mr.* Fowler, and, as *I--said yesterday, he-will-be-able to-tell-you-the* cost *of-the* proposed *improvement.*

Exercise 98.
Write in Shorthand.

Quinn & Fowler,
   Quincy, Ill.
*Dear-*Sirs:

Will-you please express *to us as* quickly *as*-possible five gross small bottles *of-your* liquid glue? *We-are--surprised your* traveler *has* missed *us* since last *January. We-*suppose *he-has-been* nowhere near our town, or *he--would-have* given *us a call.*

                        Yours-truly,

Exercise 99.
Write in Shorthand.

1. Wolf, wolves, unwell, unwilling, willingness.
2. Wheels, where, whine, whisper, whisker.
3. Tearer, steerer, clearer, sneerer, borer, jeerer.
4. Scholar, foiler, viler, insular, chancellor.
5. Scamp, romp, shampoo, imbued, ambush.
6. Hamper, bequeath, quibble, quire, iniquity.
7. *We-are* mailing *you-the* stamps *to-*day.
8. *At-your-*request *we-will go to-the* inquest.
9. Where *can-we* obtain *a* ruler like *Mr.* Wiley's?
10. *If-you-are* unwell, *or* unwilling *to-go, you-may* stay away.
11. *They ought to-*impose *a* heavy fine.
12. *He* struck *me with an* unwieldy bamboo.
13. *It-would-be* fairer *to* obtain *a* fresh shearer.

LESSON 22.

TICK AND DOT *H*.

88. It has already been explained (paragraph 15) that the *downward h* is employed when *h stands alone* or is followed by a simple *k* or *g*; and that in most other cases the *upward* form of *h* is written. When the stroke *h* is used medially, care must be taken to write the circle of the *h* so that it cannot be mistaken for the circle *s*; thus ⟨⟩ *behave*, ⟨⟩ *adhere*, ⟨⟩ *unholy*, ⟨⟩ *unhook*, ⟨⟩ *Mohawk*.

89. The downward *h* is contracted to a mere *tick* before) ⌒ ((upward) and ⟩, and before the heavy letters,) ⌒ and ⟩ ; thus ⟨⟩ *home*, ⟨⟩ *hale*, ⟨⟩ *hair*, ⟨⟩ *hemp*, ⟨⟩ *hearer*. The tick is prefixed to)) only when they are followed by a final vowel, as ⟨⟩ *hussy*, ⟨⟩ *hazy*. Where convenient, the tick *h* may also be prefixed to a straight downstroke hooked for *r*; thus ⟨⟩ *Hebrew*, ⟨⟩ *hydra*, ⟨⟩ *hedger*. The tick *h* is always read *first*, and it is *never* used in the *middle* of a word. It may, however, be employed medially in *phrases*; thus ⟨⟩ *in her own*, ⟨⟩ *we have her own*, ⟨⟩ *of her*, ⟨⟩ *to her*, ⟨⟩ *to hear the*.

90. When the stroke *h* would be inconvenient, the aspirate may be expressed by a light *dot*, placed *before* the vowel which is to be aspirated; thus ⟨⟩ *manhood*, ⟨⟩ *loophole*, ⟨⟩ *misapprehension*, ⟨⟩ *downhill*.

Exercise 100.

Read, copy, and transcribe.

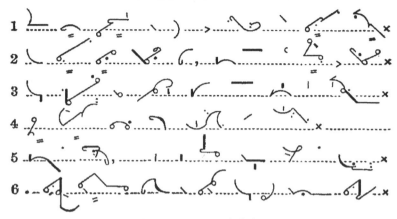

Exercise 101.

Read, copy, and transcribe.

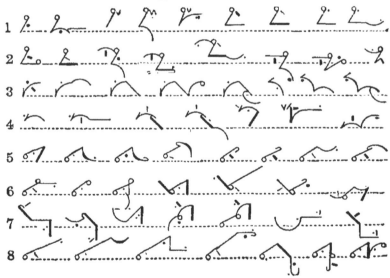

Exercise 102.

Write in Shorthand.

1. Hue, hoe, hoax, hock, hag, hogs.
2. Hall, hull, helper, heal, whole, wholesome.
3. Hire, hirer, herb, hark, hearty, harness.
4. Whom, humane, humanity, hemp, hempen.
5. Hussy, heater, hitherto, hyperbole.
6. Upholster, incoherence, adhesion, boyhood.

7. *Mr.* Henry Hopkins,
    Austin, Tex.
Dear-Sir:

In-reply-*to-your*-favor *of* January 8th, *we-have-the--pleasure to* enclose-herewith sample *of a* stain *which-will give your* mahogany *a very* rich hue. *We-have-no* apprehension *of* failure *in-your* case, *because we-do a* big wholesale business *in-this* stain, *which-is-in very general* use. Joiners, upholsterers, *and others*, use *it to* heighten *the* effect *when* finishing *high*-class jobs, *and-we-can* assure *you-the* stain *always* turns *out* well. *We*-trust *to*-hear *from-you when you have given-the* sample *a* test.

Very truly-yours,

CONTRACTIONS.

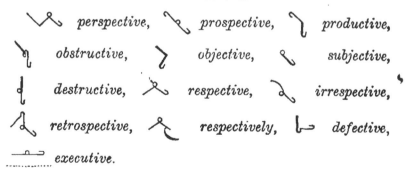

94   COURSE IN ISAAC PITMAN SHORTHAND.

Exercise 103.

Read, copy, and transcribe.

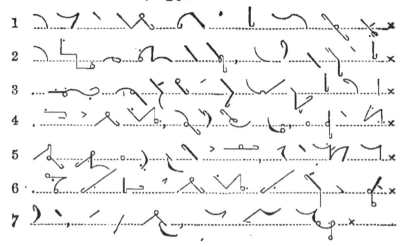

Exercise 104.

Write in Shorthand.

1. *There-is-nothing* admirable *in-the obstructive ways of-the respective* parties, *and-they-are* both *given to retrospective* wisdom.

2. *You know your objective, and you see how* necessary *a knowledge of perspective will-be, if-you-are to-*please *the executive.*

3. *They*-were *one and all* advised *to-give up their destructive ways, and to-*repair *the defective* property.

4. *The* speaker said *we-were all and each respectively* liable *to* prosecution, *if our* counsel *was productive of-*trouble.

5. *The subjective* test *was by-no-*means properly taken, *and-we-shall* ask-*the executive to* insist *upon a more* thorough examination, *irrespective of-the* teacher's opinion.

6. *The* sketch shows *the* man's possession *of* taste, *but it* also proves *his defective knowledge of perspective and a* lack *of-*training.

PHRASEOGRAMS.

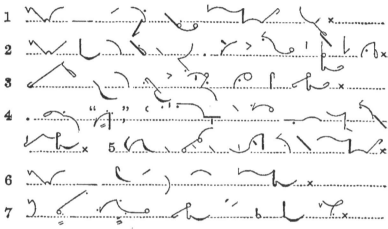

I hope you will, *Monday morning,* *Tuesday afternoon,* *yesterday afternoon,* *Wednesday evening.*

Exercise 105.

Read, copy, and transcribe.

Exercise 106.

Write in Shorthand.

J. Heaton & Sons,
  Omaha, Nebr.
*Dear-*Sirs:

*I-*beg *to* ask *your* attention *to-the* enclosed price--list *and* illustrations *of-my high-*pressure hydraulic pump, *and-I-hope-you-will-*favor *me by* a close examination *of-the* same. Should *there-be any* likelihood *of-your* being *in-this* neighborhood *during-the next* month, *I-hope-you-will* give *me a* call, when *I-shall-be* happy *to* show *you-the* new pruning hook *Mr.* Heaton spoke *of on* Tuesday-afternoon last.
                          Very-truly-yours,

LESSON 23.

UPWARD AND DOWNWARD L.

91. At the beginning of a word, *l* is generally written upward; but when *preceded* by a *vowel*, and *followed by a simple horizontal* letter, it is written *downward;* so that a downward *l* in such cases indicates the presence of an initial vowel; thus ⌒ *alike,* but ⌒ *like;* ⌒ *along,* but ⌒ *long;* ⌒ *elm,* but ⌒ *lamb.*

92. At the end of a word, *l* is generally written upward; but *after* ⌒ ⌒ ⌒ ⌒ , and *any straight upstroke,* it is written *downward if not followed by a vowel;* so that a downward *l* in such cases indicates the absence of a final vowel; thus ⌒ *full,* but ⌒ *fully;* ⌒ *vale,* but ⌒ *valley;* ⌒ *scale,* but ⌒ *scaly;* ⌒ *squall,* but ⌒ *squally;* ⌒ *yell,* but ⌒ *yellow.*

93. Final *l* is always written downward after ⌒ and ⌒ ; thus ⌒ *nail,* ⌒ *only,* ⌒ *wrongly.*

94. The compound consonant ⌐ *rer* is used where downward *r* may be used; thus ⌒ *fair,* ⌒ *fairer;* but ⌒ *aspire,* ⌒ *aspirer.*

95. The compound consonant ⌐ *ler* is used after those letters which would be followed by a *downward l;* thus ⌒ *fuller,* ⌒ *valor,* ⌒ *scaler,* ⌒ *squaller,* ⌒ *ruler;* while the sign ⌒ (*lr*) is used after those letters which would be followed by an upward *l;* thus

UPWARD AND DOWNWARD "L."

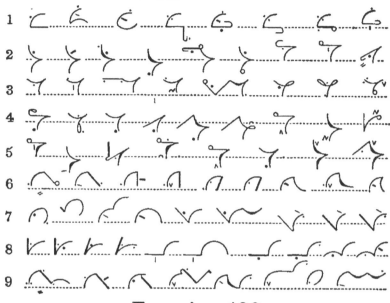

paler, tiller, jailer, cooler, molar.

The student should also refer again to paragraph 38.

Exercise 107.

Read, copy, and transcribe.

Exercise 108.

Write in Shorthand.

1. Elmira, Illinois, Alleghany, Allentown, Los Angeles.
2. Dansville, Knoxville, Jacksonville, Peekskill, Jonesville.
3. Newly, Manila, exceedingly, voiceless, facile.
4. Veal, admiral, yell, prevail, Seville, willingly.
5. Veil, fuel, fill, filler, foil, foiler, dual, Powell.
6. Deal, dealer, tall, taller, boil, boiler, pale, paler.
7. Atlanta, Alaska, Lincoln, Lancaster, Altoona.
8. Lexington, Lima, Milton, Toledo, Alpine, Salem.
9. Follow, volley, villa, rally, yellow, villain, felon.
10. Family, sickly, leisurely, loosely, Brazil, heavily.

7 S. C.

98 COURSE IN ISAAC PITMAN SHORTHAND.

CONTRACTIONS AND GRAMMALOGUES.

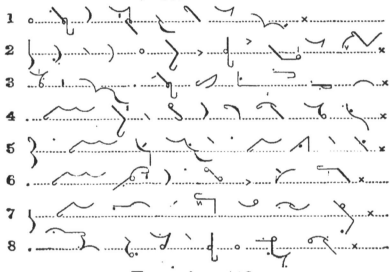

abstraction, obstruction, subjection, objection, destruction, uniform-ity-ly, unanimity-ous.

Exercise 109.

Read, copy, and transcribe.

Exercise 110.

Write in Shorthand.

1. *What objection can you have to-the obstruction* proposed?
2. *We owe our advance to-the uniformity of-the lessons.*
3. *The subjection of-the enemy and-the destruction of-his* ships were-only possible *by* strenuous labor.
4. *His abstraction led to on obstruction on-the* line.
5. *We-are unanimous in-our-opinion as-to-the* loss *of-the* vessel.
6. *The uniformity of-his-life led to-his* election *as* head *of-the Executive.*

7. *I-hope-you-will* induce *them to*-remove-*the obstruction*.
8. *He* gave lessons *to-the* boy *in architecture and architectural* design.

Exercise 111.

Write in Shorthand.

E. Lawson & Sons,
    Toledo, Ohio.
Dear-Sirs:

In-reply-*to-your*-favor *of* June 29th, *we*-enclose--herewith quotations *for* umbrellas *of-the* style *you*--require, *and-we*-feel *sure you-will* like both-*the* appearance *and-the*-prices. *We-believe our* umbrellas *and* parasols *are* unsurpassed *for* elegance *of* design *and* finish, *as--well-as for* length *of* wear. *They-are* immensely popular wherever *they-are* sold, *because of-the* excellence *of-the* make *and-the* reasonable prices *at-which they are* produced. *We should-be*-pleased *to-tell-our* traveler *to-call--upon you if-you* desire *it*.

                             Respectfully-yours,

Exercise 112.

Write in Shorthand.

The Ellison Bicycle Store,
    Elmira, *N. Y.*
Dear-Sirs:

Referring-*to-your*-favor *of-the* 12th, *the* extra long seat pillar *for Mr.* Lonsdale's chainless bicycle *will-be*-ready *by* Friday-evening *at-the* latest, *and-will-be--delivered* early *on* Saturday-morning. *We-are* exceedingly sorry *to*-learn *of-the* trouble *you have-had through-the* delay, *but-we-can*-assure-*you it-is-impossible to* finish *the* job *any* sooner.

                             Very-truly-yours,

LESSON 24.

UPWARD AND DOWNWARD *R*.

96. The student has already learned (in paragraph 15) the general rule for the use of the upward and downward forms of *r*, and he has seen (in the same paragraph) that the object of the rule is *vowel indication*. Where, however, this object can only be gained at the sacrifice of ease in writing, experience shows that it is better to make an exception to the general rule, to disregard the vowels, and to use the outline which is more easily written, and, therefore, conducive to speed. Accordingly, it was pointed out (in paragraph 49) that *upward r* is written *after* a *straight* upstroke, and *after* a curve and circle like ⌣ or ⌣. The student is now desired to note that the *upward* form of *r* is also used, regardless of vowels, when it *precedes t, d, ch, j, th, kl, gl,* or *w,* and when it *follows ks, gs,* or *two descending* strokes; thus ―― *closer,* ―― *grocer,* ―― *aright,* ―― *arrayed,* ―― *arch,* ―― *urge,* ―― *oracle,* ―― *argal,* ―― *Irwin,* ―― *prepare,* ―― *Shakespeare,* ―― *trampler.* It will be remembered, too, that final *r* when hooked (paragraph 75) is generally written upward.

Exercise 113.

Read, copy, and transcribe.

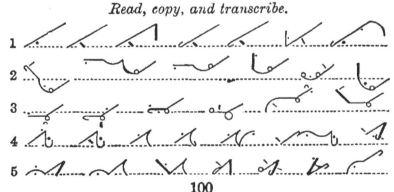

UPWARD AND DOWNWARD "R."

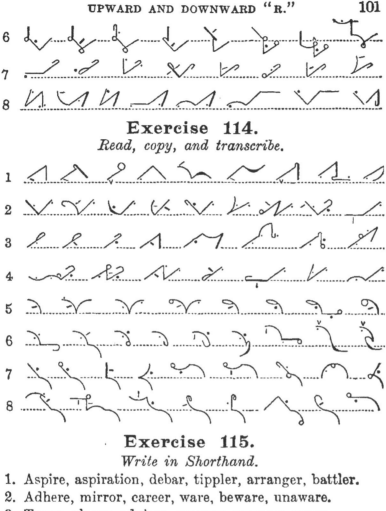

Exercise 115.
Write in Shorthand.

1. Aspire, aspiration, debar, tippler, arranger, battler.
2. Adhere, mirror, career, ware, beware, unaware.
3. Taxer, glazer, adviser, grocery, answers, **razor**.
4. Burn, morn, yarn, barn, acorn, sojourn.
5. Rye, raw, rue, reign, wreath, ridge, wrench.
6. Auricle, origination, urgency, erudition.
7. Air, airy, arm, orb, irrigation, aroma, ark.
8. Irish, irony, ironical, argue, arraign, era.
9. Jeer, injure, veer, user, shear, adore, spear.
10. Unfair, polar, inspire, severe, glare, stir, burst.
11. Barrow, tarry, ferry, fury, summary, marine.
12. Dreary, dairy, saddlery, bureau, carry, narrow.

CONTRACTIONS.

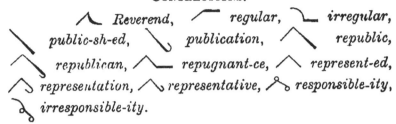

Exercise 116.

Read, copy, and transcribe.

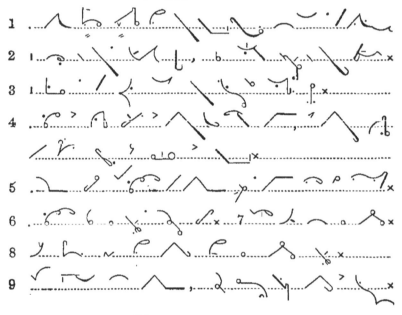

Exercise 117.

Write in Shorthand.

1. The publication was issued to-the public by-the representative of-the Rev. Arthur Rose.
2. The story of-the republic, just published, shows how-the representatives saw their responsibility and refused to be led by irresponsible men to-the admission of-the repugnant principle of taxation minus representation.

3. *Their repugnance to-the irregular* revenue *was* clearly *represented, and-the responsibility for-the*-measure thrown *upon-the regular representative of-the* taxers.
4. *We-shall publish the* speeches *of-the responsible* leaders *of-the republican* party *at-the*-close *of-the year.*

Exercise 118.
Read, copy, and transcribe.

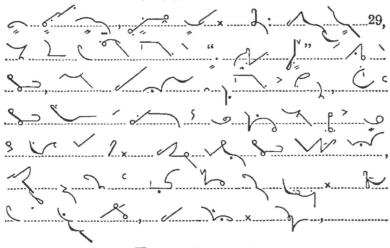

Exercise 119.
Write in Shorthand.

Murray Bros.,
    Westminster, B. C.
Dear-Sirs:

In-reply-*to-your*-favor *of January* 30th, *we-regret we-have-been* unable *to*-place-*the* cargo *of* spruce refuse *to-which-you*-refer, *and-we*-fear *there-is-no* likelihood *of-our* obtaining *a buyer* just-now. *We*-were *in* hopes *of--*success *yesterday*-morning, *but-the* party refuses *to--*proceed *with-the* business *to-*day, *and our* exertions *have-been to no* purpose. *Should-we come* across *a* customer *to-*day *or to-*morrow *at a* reasonable price *we--will* wire *you.*

                Respectfully-yours,

LESSON 25.
REVIEW.

97. (a) The *shun* hook is written: (i.) Inside curves; (ii.) on the right side of simple *t*, *d*, or *j*; (iii.) when added to a simple straight stroke *other than t, d, or j*, on the side opposite to the last vowel; (iv.) when added to a hooked or circled straight stroke, on the side opposite to the hook or circle; (v.) on the *under* side of *k* or *g*, when these letters follow *f* or *v*; and (vi.) on the *upper* side of *k* or *g*, when these letters follow *upward l*.

(b) The *shun* hook is *not* written when *shun* is immediately preceded by a diphthong and a vowel.

(c) When following the circle *s*, the sound of *shun* is expressed by a *small* hook.

(d) The sound of *r* is added to downward *l* and downward *r* by *thickening* these letters.

(e) The sound of *p* or *b* is added to *m* by thickening the letter.

(f) A *large* initial hook adds *w* to *k* or *g*.

(g) A *large* initial hook adds *wh* to upward *l*, while a *small* initial hook adds *w* to the same letter.

(h) The aspirate *h* is added to *w* by enlarging the hook of the letter.

(i) *H* is expressed by a *tick* before)) ⌒ ⌒ ⌒ ⟍ ⟍ , and before the straight down-strokes hooked for *r*.

(j) When the stroke *h* is not convenient in the middle of a word, the aspirate may be indicated by placing a *dot* before the vowel sign.

(k) An *initial vowel* may be *indicated* in such words as *alike, along*, by writing the *downward l*; while a *final vowel* may be *indicated* in such words as *fully, scaly*, by writing the *upward l*.

REVIEW. 105

(*l*) As a rule, *downward r* is written when a word *begins with a vowel* followed by *r*; while *upward r* is written if a word *ends with a vowel* preceded by *r*; but to avoid an awkward outline, *either r* is written, irrespective of vowel.

Exercise 120.

Read, copy, and transcribe.

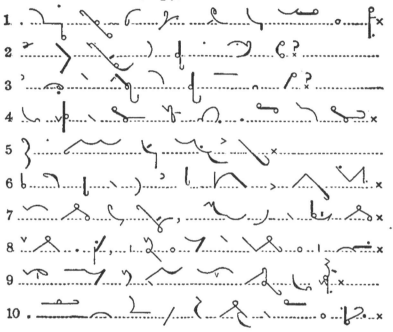

Exercise 121.

Write in Shorthand.

1. *The* arrival *of-our* representative *was altogether unexpected*.
2. *The regular* source *of-his* supplies *was insignificant*.
3. *The* new taxation *will* swell *the public* revenue.
4. *We wish the* physician *to-*make *a subjective and objective* examination *of-*her eyes.

5. *The representative of-the* ruler wore *a uniform of-* -gray.
6. *The* superscription *was a* miserable scrawl.
7. *The* discussion *was productive of a significant* increase *in-the* subscriptions.
8. *Your* views *may-be repugnant to-the executive and-the* regular members *of-the* club.

Exercise 122.
Write in Shorthand.

James Perry & Co.,
    Jacksonville, Fla.
*Dear-*Sirs:

If-you have-the least notion *of an* alteration *in-the* situation *of-your* business premises, *we should* like *you to-call and-inspect-the* new suite *of* offices *we-have-*just *put up on* Fifth Avenue. *There-can-be no* better position *in-the-*city *for a* business like *yours, and-we should-be- -*pleased *to* arrange *an* early lease *at* favorable rates.

    Yours-respectfully,

Exercise 123.
Write in Shorthand.

Mr. Thomas Batty,
    Chicago, Ill.
*Dear-*Sir:

In response *to-your* inquiry, *we-have-the-pleasure to* enclose-herewith specimen pages *of-our* new "Star Library," *with* prices *of-the* books already *published. We should-be-*pleased *to-deliver-the* whole set *to-you on* receipt *of half-the* published price, *the other half to be* paid *within* six-months *of-delivery; or, if-you* prefer *it, we-can* make *a* liberal reduction *for* cash.

    Yours-truly,

LESSON 26.

THE HALVING PRINCIPLE.

98. (*a*) Halving a *light* consonant indicates the addition of *t;* thus ⌐ *pack,* ⌐ *packed;* ⌐ *tree,* ⌐ *treat,* ⌐ *treats,* ⌐ *streets;* ⌐ *play,* ⌐ *plate,* ⌐ *plates.*

(*b*) Halving a *heavy* consonant indicates the addition of *d;* thus ⌐ *grey,* ⌐ *grade,* ⌐ *grades;* ⌐ *brew,* ⌐ *brewed,* ⌐ *broods;* ⌐ *rub,* ⌐ *rubbed.*

(*c*) A consonant which is *finally* hooked, or has a finally-joined diphthong, or which occurs in a word of *more than one syllable*, may (with rare exceptions) be halved to indicate the addition of *either t* or *d;* thus ⌐ *pain,* ⌐ *paint* or *pained,* ⌐ *paints;* ⌐ *men,* ⌐ *mend* or *meant,* ⌐ *mends;* ⌐ *wave,* ⌐ *waved,* ⌐ *waft,* ⌐ *wafts;* ⌐ *painted;* ⌐ *credit;* ⌐ *proud,* ⌐ *feud.* ⌐ *rapid;* ⌐ *colored.*

Exercise 124.
Read, copy, and transcribe.

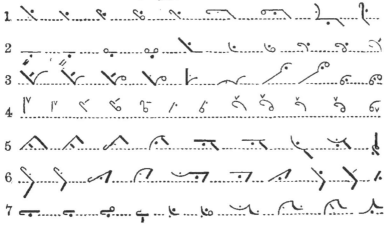

Exercise 125.

Write in Shorthand.

1. Lay, late, colt, pelt, tacked, decked, fight.
2. Enjoy, enjoyed, dodged, jade, goad, goads, dragged.
3. Shot, shots, night, caught, cut, cuts, bud, buds.
4. Spy, spite, stray, straight, mate, mates, notes.
5. Dry, dried, dread, broad, blade, blades, bread.
6. Pen, penned, spend, spends, gain, gained, grained.
7. Grant, grants, lend, lends, fine, find, finds.
8. Shaded, shredded, plated, skated, melted, related.

99. (a) Strokes of unequal length must not be joined unless the junction is clearly shown; thus ⟋ *checked*, ⟋ *named*; but ⟋ *cooked*, ⟋ *animate*.

(b) Half-sized *t* or *d*, immediately following the consonant *t* or *d*, is always *disjoined*; thus ⟋ *treated*, ⟋ *dreaded*, ⟋ *traded*, ⟋ *edited*.

100. Half-sized *w* (⌒) is used as a contraction for the termination *ward*, *wart*, *wort*, and half-sized *y* (⌒) for *yard*; thus ⟋ *backward*, ⟋ *stalwart*, ⟋ *dockyard*.

101. *Final t* or *d*, when followed by a *sounded vowel*, must be *written in full*; thus ⟋ *fault*, but ⟋ *faulty*.

102. There is no *third position* for words whose outlines consist of half-sized letters only, or of horizontal letters joined to half-sized letters. When the vowel or principal vowel in such words is a third-place vowel, the outline is written in the *second position*; thus ⟋ *tend*, ⟋ *splint*, ⟋ *kilt*, ⟋ *colt*, ⟋ *meted*.

THE HALVING PRINCIPLE.

Exercise 126.
Read, copy, and transcribe.

Exercise 127.
Write in Shorthand.

1. Doubted, doted, credited, obtruded, imitated.
2. Roast, roasted, arrested, fasted, dusted, lasted.
3. Downward, southward, rearward, stock-yard.
4. Pit, pity, body, giddy, mite, mighty, witty.
5. Rain, rained, rent, rents, learnt, parent.
6. Cough, coughed, craft, crafts, vent, vents.
7. Lodged, bridged, waged, grudged, hinged, dredged.
8. Patted, sifted, wounded, indeed, sounded.
9. Print, prints, tint, tints, wound, wounds.

GRAMMALOGUES.

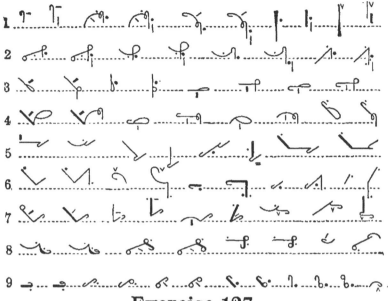

quite, — could, accord-ing or according to or cart, cared, guard, great, called, cold or equalled, gold, cannot, gentleman, gentlemen, happened, particular, opportunity, child. not.

Exercise 128.

Read, copy, and transcribe.

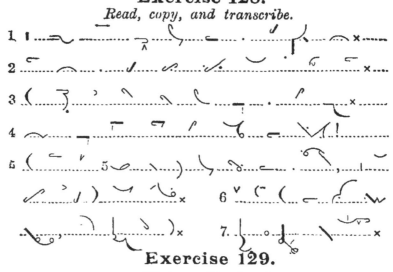

Exercise 129.

Write in Shorthand.

1. *I-cannot quite see how-the gentleman could-have called* sooner.
2. *The particular* account *you* name *shall-be* settled *on-the* first opportunity.
3. *I-happened to be in when-the child* changed *the* note *for gold.*
4. He had a *great* coat *to guard him, so he cared nothing for-the cold.*
5. *We-cannot-be* wrong *in according-the gentleman a* hospitable reception *on-this particular opportunity.*
6. *The* men stood *on guard* beside-*the great cart, which--was* loaded *with gold for-the* bank.
7. *If-this-gentleman's* talents *had equalled his* audacity, *I-know-not what* might *have happened.*
8. *The* little *child* knelt *down and* asked-*the great* God *to guard him through-the* dreaded night.
9. *The gentleman had a* rooted *objection to-the-*treatment *he* received.

103. The halving principle is employed for the indication of the words *it, not, word* and *would,* in phrases like the following: .... I am not, ... I do not or I had

THE HALVING PRINCIPLE. 111

not, *I did not,* *you may not,* *you are not,* *you were not,* *you will not,* *I hope you will not,* *if it,* *if it has (or is),* *in which it is (or has) this word,* *we would be.*

Exercise 130.

Read, copy, and transcribe.

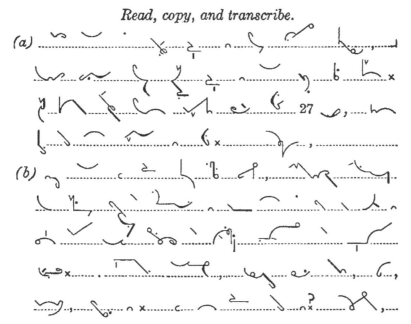

Exercise 131.

Write in Shorthand.

Mr. Edward Hunt,
  Cleveland, Ohio.

Dear-Sir:

We-desire *to-call your* attention *to-the* enclosed sample *of* Fruit-Salt, *which-we-think-you-may-not know.* As *will-be* observed, *the* bottle *in-which-it-is* packed *is a* very pretty one, *and-we* anticipate *a* big demand *for-the* article *when-it-is* displayed *in-your* store. We *should-be-*-glad *to-*hear *if-it* meets *with your* approval, *and-we-are-*-sure *you-will-not-be* wrong *in* placing *it on-your* list. Prices *of-the different* sizes enclosed.

  Respectfully-yours,

LESSON 27.

THE HALVING PRINCIPLE (Concluded).

104. The four consonants ⌒ ⌣ ⌒ ⌒ , besides being halved for the addition of *t*, may be halved and *thickened* to indicate the addition of *d*; thus ⌒ *palmed*, ⌒ *mode*, ⌒ *aimed*; ⌒ *designed*, ⌒ *sound*, ⌒ *snowed*; ⌒ *piled*, ⌒ *old*; ⌒ *shared*, ⌒ *erred*, ⌒ *hoard*.

105. The signs ⌒ *ld* (written *downward*) and ⌒ *rd* are *not* used if a sounded vowel comes between the *l-d* or *r-d*. In such cases, the consonants must be written in full; thus ⌒ *paled*, but ⌒ *pallid*; ⌒ *bowled*, but ⌒ *ballad*; ⌒ *paired*, but ⌒ *parried*; ⌒ *tarred*, but ⌒ *tarried*.

106. The consonants ⌒ *mp*, ⌣ *ng*, cannot be halved to express the addition of *t* or *d*, unless they are hooked initially or finally; thus ⌒ *slumber*, ⌒ *slumbered*; ⌒ *impugn*, ⌒ *impugned;* ⌒ *canker*, ⌒ *cankered*. The double consonants ⌒ *lr* ⌒ *rr* cannot be *halved* to indicate the addition of *t* or *d*, under any circumstances, because the signs ⌒ ⌒ are utilized for the representation of *ld* and *rd* respectively. Write *ist upward* in ⌒ *salvationist*, etc.

107. The half-length *r* [⌒] must *never* be written alone, nor with final *s* only added. Words like ⌒ *rate*, ⌒ *writes*, are, therefore, written in full. The final

THE HALVING PRINCIPLE.

sound of *rt* is generally expressed by the half-length *upstroke*, while the final sound of *rd* is, as a rule, expressed by the half-length *downstroke*; thus ⌄ *part*, ⌄ *pared*, ⌊ *dart*, ⌊ *dared*. Where it is not convenient, however, to write ⌐, the light half-length upstroke may be employed for the expression of the heavy sound; thus ⌒ *lard*, ⌒ *lured*, ⌒ *geared*.

Exercise 132.

Read, copy, and transcribe.

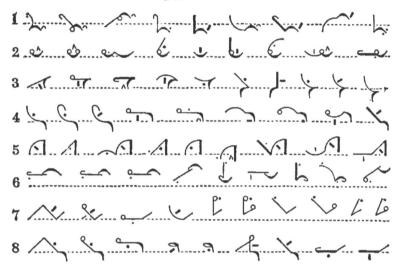

Exercise 133.

Write in Shorthand.

1. *Be* assured *you-will* repeat *the* sound results achieved *by* thousands.
2. *We-have* mailed *you* a sample copy *of* part three *of-our* new monthly.
3. *We*-enclose rate card, *and would* ask-*you to* note *this*- -point: *the* circulation *of-the* paper *is* insured *by-its* value.

COURSE IN ISAAC PITMAN SHORTHAND.

4. *We-have* presumed *to-*send *you* details *of-our* new **patent**, *and-it-would* afford *us great-pleasure to* add *your* **name** *to-our* list *of* subscribers.

5. *May-we* point-*out to-you why our* paper *is* read *by* thousands *of-the* class *it-is* desired *to-*reach?

6. *On our* part, *we-are* prepared *to-do our* best until *the* difficulty *is* conquered.

7. *We* see-*the* impending struggle, *but with your* help *we--shall* conquer, hard *though-the* task *may-be.*

8. *We* write *to* say *we* followed *your* counsel, *and-the* business *was* allowed *to-*proceed.

GRAMMALOGUES.

build-*ing* or *able to*, told or *till it*, tried, toward or *trade*, did not, had not or *do not*, chaired, cheered, *if it*, *that*, *without*, third, sent, somewhat, short, met, meeting.

Exercise 134.

Read, copy, and transcribe.

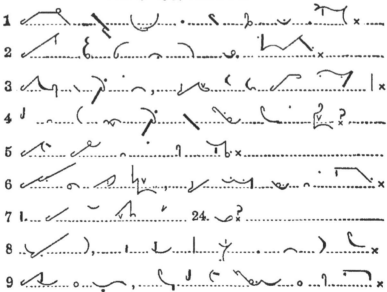

THE HALVING PRINCIPLE. 115

Exercise 135.

Write in Shorthand.

1. *Will-you not be-able-to come to-the meeting when-the* store *is* closed? Tom *was chaired at-the* last *one.*
2. *If-it-is* possible, *I-will come in for a short-*time.
3. *He-told them that without a* doubt *he-would* send *a* check *to-*day, *and-this cheered them.*
4. *We-tried to-*find *out-the* extent *of-his trade, but-we-did--not* succeed.
5. *We-*thought-*you-*might *go to see him on-the* third.
6. *We-*did send *him a* colored piece, *but it-was somewhat different from-the* pattern *he-sent.*

PHRASEOGRAMS.

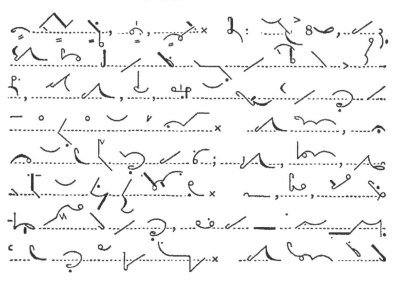

Exercise 136.

Read, copy, and transcribe.

Exercise 137.

Write in Shorthand.

Mr. Edward Hindley,
    Sandford, Ill.
Dear-Sir:

In-reply-*to-your*-favor *of-the* 30th ult., *we would*-say *that-we-are,* at-*all*-times, *willing to*-replace *any*-part *of a* bedstead *which-may-be-*found damaged *on-delivery, if-it-*-is quite-clear *that-the* fault *is ours.* *You-may-*rest assured *that all-our* bedsteads *are* built *of-the* finest steel *and* iron, *and-that every care is* taken *to see that-the* goods *are* right *when sent out of-the* factory. At-*the*-same-time, *it-may* happen, *from*-time-*to-*time, *that* some latent flaw *may-be* discovered *when a* bedstead *has* left *our* place, *in-which-*case *we-are-*only *too-*glad *to-*remedy *the* defect, *and-thus* show *our* earnest desire *to-*turn *out* absolutely sound goods. Please indicate *the* faulty part, *and-we-will* forward *one to-*replace *it.*

Yours-respectfully,

LESSON 28.

THE DOUBLING PRINCIPLE.

108. Curved consonants are doubled in length to indicate the addition of *tr, dr,* or *thr* (heavy); thus ⌒ *laughter,* ⌒ *lender,* ⌒ *another,* ⌒ *mother.* (See paragraph 113.)

109. Straight consonants with an initial circle, or with a final hook or finally-joined diphthong, or following another stroke, are doubled in length to indicate the addition of *tr, dr* or *thr;* thus ⟍ *painter,* | *tender,* ⟋ *rafter,* ⟍ *captor,* ⟶ *counter.*

110. The character ⌒ is doubled in length to express the addition of *r;* thus ⌒ *pamper,* ⌒ *temper.* ⌒ *chamber;* while the character ⌣ is doubled in length to indicate the addition of *kr* or *gr;* thus ⌣ *shrinker,* ⌣ *longer.* It is, however, generally more convenient to use the signs ⌒ and ⌣ in verbs, because they can be readily halved for the past tense; as ⌒ *clamber,* ⌒ *clambered,* ⌣ *conquer,* ⌣ *conquered.* The hooked forms ⌣ ⌒ may be doubled in length for the addition of the syllable *-er;* thus ⌣ *linger,* ⌣ *lingerer,* ⌒ *lumber,* ⌒ *lumberer.*

111. In very common words, where there is no likelihood of clashing, it is allowable to make a letter double length to express the addition of *-ture;* thus ⌣ *feature,* ⌣ *signature,* ⌣ *picture.*

112. Final *tr, dr*, or *thr*, when followed by a vowel, must be *written*, and not *indicated* by doubling; thus ⌒ *flatter*, but ⌒ *flattery*; ⌒ *cinder*, but ⌒ *cindery*; ⌒ *signature*, but ⌒ *signatory*.

113. The double-length ⌒, when *standing alone*, or with a final circle only added, is reserved for the representation of *light sounds*; thus ⌒ *letter*, ✓ *alter*; words like ⌒ *leader*, ⌒ *ladder*, ⌒ *leather*, being written as here shown.

114. When the present tense of a verb is written with the double-length principle, the past tense is writtten with the half-length principle; *thus* ⌒ *matter*, ⌒ *mattered*; ⌒ *ponder*, ⌒ *pondered* ⌒ *canter*, ⌒ *cantered*; ⌒ *winter*, ⌒ *wintered*, ⌒ *loiter*, ⌒ *loitered*.

115. Double-length *downstrokes* have only the *third* position, through the line; thus ⌒ *plunder*, ⌒ *splendor*, ⌒ *tender*, ⌒ *asunder*. Double-length horizontal letters take *two positions* only; thus ⌒ *matter*, ⌒ *motor* or *meter*; ⌒ *canter*, ⌒ *counter*. Double-length upstrokes may be written in any of the three positions, in accordance with the rules governing the position of outlines. (See pars. 7, 13, and 18.)

Exercise 138.

Read, copy, and transcribe.

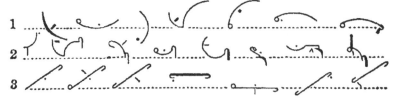

THE DOUBLING PRINCIPLE

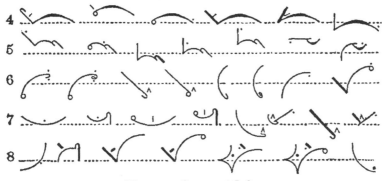

Exercise 139.

Write in Shorthand.

1. Mender, slander, slender, flounders, borders, remainder.
2. Calendar, folders, fathers, knitters, flitters.
3. Disasters, stimulator, litters, oyster, barters.
4. Stamper, stampers, thumper, moulder, orders.
5. Banter, banters, grafter, rafters, printers.
6. Elector, electors, protector, chapters, numerator.
7. Render, renders, rendered, blenders, pandered.
8. Slaughtered, sweltered, feathery, gentry, wondered.

GRAMMALOGUES AND CONTRACTIONS.

spirit, may not, hand, under, yard, word, wonderful-ly.

Exercise 140.

Read, copy, and transcribe.

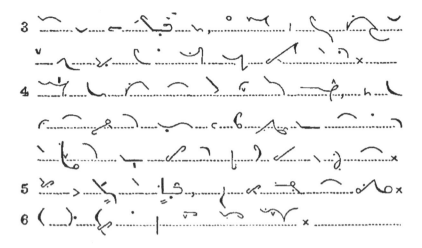

Exercise 141.

Write in Shorthand.

1. *They*-want *to know why he*-went *to* Lincoln City and showed *his hand.*

2. *If-this-is-the* spirit *in-which-you* speak *of-the* secret, *it*-won't-*be* long ere *it-is*-known *to all.*

3. *I*-fear *it-is-not your* nature *to be* quiet; *but* unless *you-are more* prudent *you-will* yet *have to*-repent some rash *word.*

4. *You-are wonderfully* outspoken, *and-not a yard will I*-move until *I-see-you under-the care of-the* inspector.

Phraseograms.

116. In accordance with the preceding rules, the doubling principle is employed in phraseography for the indication of the words *there, their;* thus (a) In stroke logograms, as in ⁀ *in their,* ⁀ *can be there,* ⁀ *upon their,* ⁀ *has to be there;* (b) In outlines that are not logograms as ⁀ *I have seen their.*

Exercise 142.

Read, copy, and transcribe.

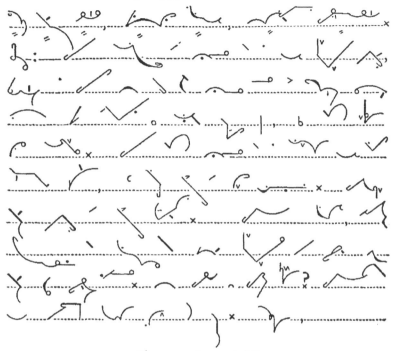

Exercise 143.

Write in Shorthand.

Mr. John Henderson,
   Nome, Alaska.
Dear-Sir:

*We-have-your-*letter *of-*March 24th, *and-we-shall* order--*the* cylinder bolts *from-the* factory before-*there-is* time *for-the-other* parts *of-the* machinery *to-come* forward. *We-know-there-is* an extra rush *of-*orders just-now, *but-we--think-there-is-no* likelihood *of-your-*order being delayed. *If-there-is-the* least indication *of-*such *a thing we-will-see to-it that* less pressing jobs *are put* aside, *so-that nothing shall* hinder *the* finishing *of-your gold* mining machinery *by-the* promised date.   *Very-truly-yours,*

LESSON 29.

VOCALIZATION OF DOUBLE CONSONANTS.

117. To obtain a good outline, the double consonants of the *pl* and *pr* series may be employed even though an accented vowel comes between the two consonants. If the intervening vowel is a dot vowel, it is expressed by writing a small circle AFTER the consonant stroke for a *long* or *short vowel;* thus ⌒ *careless,* ⌒ *chairman,* ⌒ *cheers,* ⌒ *dark.*

118. An intervening dash vowel, or a diphthong, is expressed by writing the vowel or diphthong sign THROUGH the consonant stroke; thus ⌒ *Baltimore,* ⌒ *mixture.* When, however, an initial or final hook or circle would interfere with the intersection of the vowel-sign, the latter may be written at the BEGINNING of the consonant for a first-place vowel or diphthong, and at the END for a third-place vowel of diphthong; thus ⌒ *corporal,* ⌒ *figuration;* also when the general rule of placing the circle is awkward of application, the circle may be written before the stroke; thus, ⌒ *flashily.*

119. The methods of vocalizing the double consonants provide the writer with an additional means of distinguishing words in *-tor* from words in *-ture;* thus ⌒ *captor,* ⌒ *capture.*

GRAMMALOGUES.

⌒ school, ⌒ schooled.

Exercise 144.

Read, copy, and transcribe.

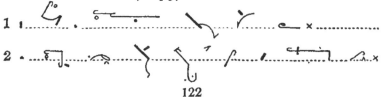

VOCALIZATION OF DOUBLE CONSONANTS

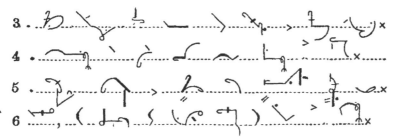

Exercise 145.
Write in Shorthand.

Mr. Charles Reid,
    Oxford, Mass.
Dear-Sir:

*I-have-your-*favor *of-the* 24th *inst., and-I-*find *that-the-*terms *you* propose *are, on-the* whole, reasonable. *Your* calculation *of-*profits, *however, is* palpably wrong *in--one* instance, *as you-will-see on* further-examination. *You-will* recollect *that-it-will-be* necessary *for-you to-*cultivate *the* trade *in-your* district. *My* former *representative was* culpably *careless towards-the* end *of-his* engagement, *and-the* business *will* require *a* little nursing *for a* time. *I-*am-perfectly *sure, however, that a* display *of* energy *by a* sharp man *of* persuasive *talents, and a* judicious distribution *of-the* literature *I-will* send *you, will* soon encourage *a* return *of-the* former extensive sales. Please *call* here *on-*Thursday *to-*sign-*the* agreement.   *Yours-truly,*

Exercise 146.
Read, copy, and transcribe.

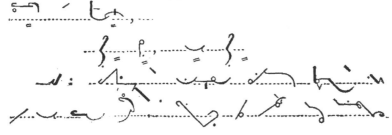

124 COURSE IN ISAAC PITMAN SHORTHAND.

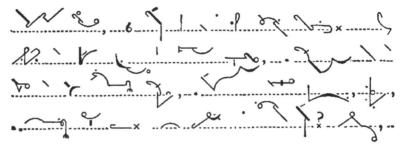

CONTRACTIONS.

⸺ commercial, ⌣ financial, ⟨ especial-ly,
⌣ influential, ⌣ uninfluential,
⟨ substantial-ly, ⟨ unsubstantial-ly, ⟨ controversy-sial, ∫ circumstance, ⌣ circumstantial,
⌢ immediate, ⌢ immediately, ⟩ prejudice-cial.

Exercise 147.

Read, copy, and transcribe.

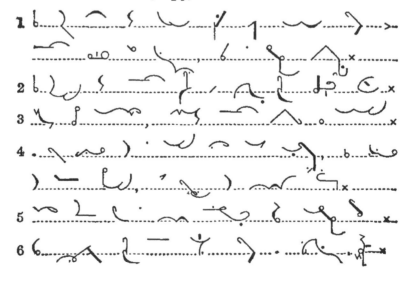

Exercise 148.
Write in Shorthand.

1. *It-is especially important that-you-should deliver-the* goods *immediately*.
2. *Any* delay *may prejudice your* chances *of*-further orders.
3. *There-is a substantial* increase *in-the financial* returns.
4. *Your immediate* attention *is* essential, *if-you would* secure-*the* business.
5. *The unsubstantial* nature *of-the commercial* traveler's resources rendered *his* chances hopeless.
6. *The circumstances* attending-*the controversy* were far *from* pleasing *to-him*.
7. *His influential* position *is* lost, *thanks to-his* insane fondness *for controversial* discussion.
8. *Oh, yes, the circumstances* were noted *immediately, but they*-were regarded *as* entirely *uninfluential*.
9. *The circumstantial* detail *of-the* narrative proved *its* accuracy.

120. Any unimportant word such as as, *the, of, or,* etc., may be omitted in a phraseogram; thus ⌒ *for (the) sake (of)*, ⌒ *more (or) less*, ⌒ *side (by) side*, etc. It is well to vocalize *him* (so that it may not clash with *me*) in such phrases as ⌒ *before him,* ⌒ *to him,* etc.

121. Judicious phrasing should be carefully cultivated by the student, as a great aid both to speed and legibility; but he should guard against the temptation to join together words which are not naturally related to one another, or which, if joined, would result in an outline extending too far from the line of writing. For additional practice in phraseography, and for further exercise in the reading of shorthand, the student is referred to "The Phonographic Phrase Book," "Selections from American Authors," and "Self-Culture," particulars of which will be found in the list at the end of the present work.

PHRASEOGRAMS.

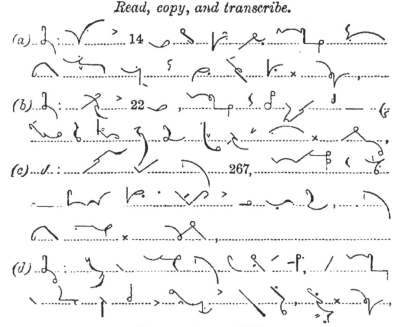

I am directed to state, I am instructed to state, I am requested to state, deliver immediately.

Exercise 149.
Read, copy, and transcribe.

Exercise 150.
Write in Shorthand.

(a) *Dear*-Sir *In*-reply-*to*-your-letter *of*-*the* 16th *inst.*, *I*-am-directed-*to*-state *that*-*there*-*is*-*no* such policy holder *on* our books. Very careful examination *has*-*been* made, *and*-*it*-*must*-*be that* your clerk *was in* error. *Respectfully*-*-yours.*

(b) *Gentlemen: I*-am-requested *to* ask *if*-*you*-*can* deliver--*immediately at* our central depot *in* New York, three *of*-*your* No. 4 Bicycles, fitted *with* Coaster Brake, *and to* ask, *if*-*you*-*are* unable *to* arrange *this*, *upon what* date *you*-*could* make *delivery? Yours*-*truly,*

LESSON 30.

DIPHONIC OR TWO-VOWEL SIGNS.

122. In many words two vowels occur consecutively, each being separately pronounced. To represent these, special signs have been provided called *diphones* (from the Greek *di* = double, and *phōnē* = a sound). In most instances, the first of the two consecutive vowels is the more important, and therefore the diphonic sign is written in the vowel-place which the first vowel would take if this occurred alone, that is, if it were not followed immediately by another vowel. The method of using the *diphones* is explained in the following rules.

123. The *diphone* ⌐ is written as follows:—

(a) In the first vowel-place to represent the vowel *ah* or *ă* and any vowel immediately following; thus ⌐ sah*i*b, ⌐ Jud*a*ism, ⌐ ultr*a*ist.

(b) In the second vowel-place to represent *ā* or *ĕ*, and any vowel immediately following; thus ⌐ lay*er*, ⌐ la*i*ty, ⌐ betr*a*yal, ⌐ surv*e*yor.

(c) In the third vowel-place to represent *ē* or *ĭ* and any vowel immediately following; thus ⌐ r*ea*l, ⌐ r*ea*lity, ⌐ r*e*-enter, ⌐ am*i*able, ⌐ m*ea*nder, ⌐ g*eo*graphy, ⌐ g*eo*graphical, ⌐ champ*io*n, ⌐ heav*ie*st, ⌐ bur*yi*ng, ⌐ glor*iou*s, ⌐ cr*ea*tor, ⌐ cr*ea*tion, ⌐ s*e*rial.

124. The *diphone* ⌐ is written as follows:—

(a) In the first vowel-place to represent *aw* and any vowel immediately following; thus ⌐ fl*aw*y, ⌐ dr*awe*r, ⌐ dr*awi*ngs, ⌐ c*awi*ng.

128 COURSE IN ISAAC PITMAN SHORTHAND.

(b) In the second vowel-place to represent ō and any vowel immediately following; thus showy, bestowal, poet, poetical, coercion.

(c) In the third vowel-place to represent ōō and any vowel immediately following; thus bruin, brewery, Louisa, Lewis, truant.

Exercise 151.

Read, copy, and transcribe.

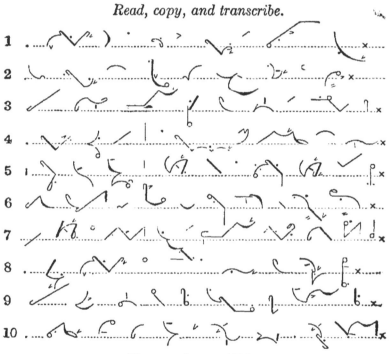

Exercise 152.

Write in Shorthand.

1. *Our* shares *have-been at a* premium *during-the* whole *of-the* period.
2. Such *a* policy *would-be* ruinous *to-our* firm *and* lead *to* disagreeable *circumstances*.

DIPHONIC OR TWO-VOWEL SIGNS. 129

3. *The* debt *is* repayable *to-the* purveyor *in* monthly instalments.
4. *The* matter *of-the* Gaiety Theatre *is-to-be* left *in* abeyance.
5. Kindly re-arrange *the* terms *and see to-the* re-insurance *of-the* theatrical costumer's premises *without* delay.
6. *Your* theory *of* minute forms *may* seem *all-right, but in* practice *you-will*-find *a* freer style *will give you* better results.
7. *The* bestowal *of-these* honors *upon-the* principal *of-the* college *and-his* coadjutor, *Mr.* Lewis Owen, *has given great-pleasure to all-their* pupils.

CONTRACTIONS.

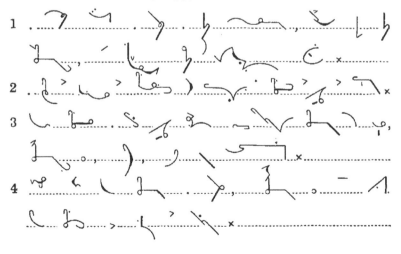

(The letter *n* is frequently omitted in the prefix *trans*.)

Exercise 153.

Read, copy, and transcribe.

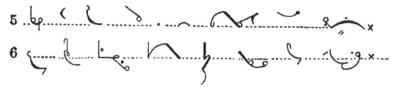

Exercise 154.
Write in Shorthand.

1. Ask-*the passenger to*-take *a messenger with him and*- -send back *the transcript of-the manuscript immediately.*
2. *The transmission of-the* transcription proved *more dangerous than-the stranger expected.*
3. *Whenever you*-write, *and whatever-the*-matter *may-be, you-should-be-able-to* read *or* transcribe *every word of-it.*
4. *You-should-understand that-there-is* danger *in* transgressing *any* rule, *and-that-the* more accurate *the* shorthand note, *the more* correct *will-be-the* transcript.
5. *I-understood that-the-*transfer *of-the* stock *was-*made *at-the-*end *of-*last September.
6. *What-is-the* nature *of-the* transgression *with-which-the* messenger is charged?

PHRASEOGRAMS.

I regard, I regret, I do not understand, your esteemed favor, I am in receipt of your esteemed favor, in reply to your esteemed favor.

Exercise 155.
Read, copy, and transcribe.

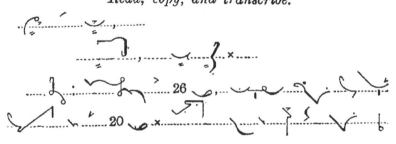

DIPHONIC OR TWO-VOWEL SIGNS.

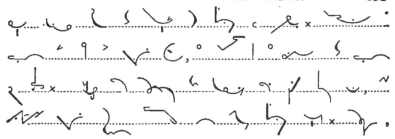

Exercise 156.

Write in Shorthand.

The Manhattan Chemical Co.,
 Brooklyn, *N. Y.*
Gentlemen:

 In-reply-*to-your*-esteemed-favor *of-yesterday,* *the* reason *why we* returned *you-the* barrel *of* zinc sulfate *was because* analysis showed *that-it-was-not* equal *to-our* sample, *and was, therefore,* quite useless *to us.* *We-do--not-under*stand *why it-was* sent, since *we*-presume *you--*were aware *that* such *a* standard *would-not* suit *our* purpose *at-all.* Please send *us* another barrel *immediately, and-be care*ful *to see that-it-is* exactly *what we* ordered.

 Very-truly-yours,

LESSON 31.

W AND Y DIPHTHONGS.

125. When the sound of *w* or *y* (or *ĭ*) is followed by a vowel, long or short, and a *diphthong* is formed, it is represented by a small semicircle; thus

wah	⊂⊃	waw		yah	⌒⌒	yaw
wā	⊂⊃	wō		yā	⌣⌣	yō
wē	⊂⊃	wōō		yē	⌣⌣	yōō

126. The semicircle is written in the place which the vowel forming the second element in the diphthong would take if it occurred alone; thus

⟨.... *Zouave*, ...⟩. *assuage*, ...⟩. *sea-weed*, ⌒ *chamois*, ...⌒ *misquote*, ⌒........ *lamb's-wool*, ...⟩ *Spaniard*, ⌣⌣. *spaniel*, ⟩⌣ *yearling*, ⟨....⟩ *Avignon*, ...⌒ *million*, ...⌒ *misyoked*, ...⌣ *question*, ...⟨ *accuse*.

127. The semicircles and their uses will be better remembered if the student observes that the SIDES of the circle ⊂⊃ represent the *w* diphthongs and the lower and upper halves ⌣⌢ represent the *y* diphthongs.

128. (*a*) The right semicircle for *waw* or *wŏ* may be joined to — ⟍ ⟋ ⎮ ∕ ⟩ ⌒ ⌒ as in .... *walk*, ⌒ *warm*, ... *warn*, ⎮ *water*, ⟩ *watcher*, ⟩ *washer*, ⌒ *Walmsley*, ... *wampum*.

"W" AND "Y" DIPHTHONGS.

(b) The right semicircle is also prefixed to ⸺ ⸺ ⌒ ⌒ as an abbreviation for *w*; thus ⸺ *woke*, ⸺ *wig*, ⸺ *women*, ⸺ *Wimpole*.

129. In proper names, the left semicircle is prefixed to downward *l*, as an abbreviation for *wĭ*; thus ⸺ *William*, ⸺ *Wilks*, ⸺ *Wilson*.

130. The joined initial semicircle is always read first, so that the abbreviated form of *w* cannot be employed in words commencing with a vowel; compare ⸺ *wake* and ⸺ *awake*; ⸺ *woke* and ⸺ *awoke*.

Exercise 157.

Read, copy, and transcribe.

Exercise 158.

Write in Shorthand.

1. *We-must* warn-*the* workman *not* to-make-*the* washers *too* tight.
2. Ask-*them to* withhold *the* order until *I-have*-seen *Mr.* Wakefield.

COURSE IN ISAAC PITMAN SHORTHAND.

3. *They* did *their* best *to* assuage *the* pain, *but-the* woman's weakness rapidly increased.
4. *There-is-no* palliation *for-the* Austrian's offence, *and--after* a brief period *in* prison, *he-will-have* to pay *the* penalty *of-his* crime.
5. *We-are-sending-the* tapioca *and-the* water-melons, *but--we-have-no* stock *of* lime-water *at-present*.
6. *All-our* paper *is* marked *with our special* water-mark.

CONTRACTIONS.

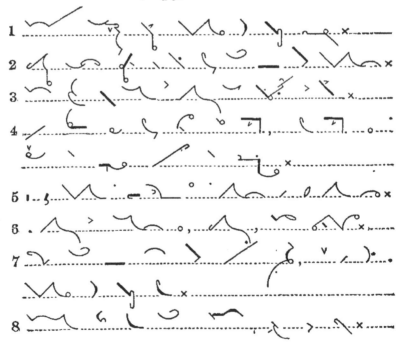

better than, rather than, rather or writer, perform-ed, performer, perform-ance, reform-ed, reformer, reforma-tion, inform-ed, informer, information, thankful, thanksgiving.

Exercise 159.

Read, copy, and transcribe.

Phraseograms.

I have to inform you, *please inform us*, *please quote us*, *please let me know*, *please let us know*, *please note*, *please forward*.

Exercise 160.
Write in Shorthand.

1. *I-have-to-inform-you that-the* report *will go* forward *by*-rail *to*-morrow.
2. Please-quote-*us for* 5,500 copies *in* typewritten fac-simile *of-the* enclosed circular.
3. Please-let-*me-know if* cotton *is* being held back *in-your* district.
4. Please-let-*us-know when you-can deliver-the* fifty bales *of* cotton, *which-are* still due.
5. Please-note-*that* bale *No.* 47 *is-no better-than-the* rest.
6. Please-forward *immediately* 30 pieces *No.* 85 Print.

Exercise 161.
Write in Shorthand.

Mr. Wm. Bryon,
    Milton, Mass.
Dear-Sir:

In-reply-*to-your*-esteemed-favor *of-the* 8th, *I-have--to-inform-you that-the* sale *of-the* property referred *to* takes-place *on-the* 26th *inst. If-you* desire further--*particulars in*-addition-*to-those given in-the* catalog enclosed, *I shall-be*-glad *to* furnish *them*. Please-note *that--there-is-no* present-intention *of* disposing *of-the* hotel *in* Ninth Avenue. *I-can,* however, *inform-you of*-some *very--good* hotel property *which-is for*-sale, *if-you care to* speculate *in-that*-direction.

    Yours-very-truly,

LESSON 32.
REVIEW.

131. (*a*) Light letters are halved for *t;* heavy letters for *d;* but a letter which is *finally* hooked, or which occurs in a word of *more than one syllable,* may be halved for *either t or d.*

(*b*) The four letters ⌒ ‿ ⌠ ⌡ may be *halved and thickened* for the addition of *d.*

(*c*) When a vowel intervenes between *l-d* or *r-d,* these letters must be written in full.

(*d*) Final *t* or *d,* followed by a sounded vowel, must be written in full.

(*e*) Half-sized *t* or *d* immediately following the letter *t* or *d,* is always *disjoined.*

(*f*) Half-sized ⁄ [✓] is written as a contraction for *ward, wart, wort,* and ⸝ for *yard.*

(*g*) The halving principle is used in phrasing to indicate the word *not, it, word, would.*

(*h*) The syllable *tr, dr,* or *thr* (and sometimes *ture*), is expressed by doubling the length of the preceding stroke.

(*i*) The character ⌒ is doubled in length for the addition of *r;* ‿ is doubled for the addition of *kr* or *gr;* ‿ ⌒ for *-er.*

(*j*) The doubling principle is used in phrasing to indicate the addition of the word *there* or *their.*

(*k*) A dot vowel may be indicated between a stroke and an *initial hook* by writing a *small circle* after the stroke.

(*l*) A dash vowel may be indicated between a stroke and an initial hook by *intersecting* the vowel sign, or, where this is not convenient, by writing the vowel sign at the *beginning* or *end* of the stroke.

(*m*) The angular signs ╱ ╲ are employed to express a vowel followed by any vowel.

(*n*) The abbreviated *w* may be prefixed to *downward l,* ― ― ⌒ ⌒

(*o*) The *w* and *y* diphthongs are expressed by a small semicircle.

REVIEW. 137

Exercise 162.
Read, copy, and transcribe.

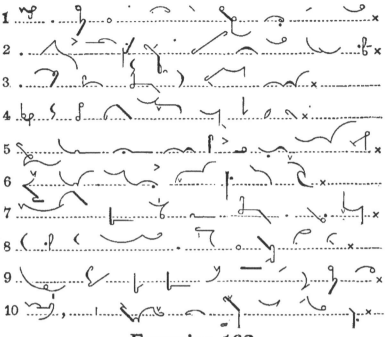

Exercise 163.
Write in Shorthand.

1. *I-hope-you-will-not-be* annoyed *at-my*-request *for*-payment.
2. *You-may-not-know that-the* influence *of-this-gentleman is* enormous.
3. *I-hope-you-are at-all*-times willing *to-do your*-best *for--the* welfare *of-the house which-you represent*.
4. *I-think-there-is* room *for* improvement *in-your* methods *of*-work.
5. *I-must* ask-*you* to be prepared, *for-there-is sure* to be *a* strict inquiry.
6. *I-am-directed to* ask-*you* to attend here *at* seven o'clock *this*-evening.
7. Please-note *that-you-are to-deliver-immediately the* goods named *in-my*-letter *of-yesterday*.
8. *Your*-esteemed favor *of-the* 4th *is* to hand, and *I-am--much*-obliged.

LESSON 33.
PREFIXES.

132. *Con-* or *com-*, when it is the first sound in a word, is expressed by a *light dot,* written at the commencement of the outline; thus ⟶ *conspire,* ⟶ *commence,* ⟶ *console,* ⟶ *commit.* Where the *con-* dot is employed, it should be the *first sign written* in the word.

133. (*a*) When the syllable *con-, com-, cum-,* or *cog-,* occurs between two consonants, it is indicated by writing the second consonant *close to* or *under* the first; thus ⟶ *inconstant,* ⟶ *disconnected,* ⟶ *recompense,* ⟶ *incumbent,* ⟶ *recognize.* The rule may also be applied to phrases; thus ⟶ *you will comply,* ⟶ *I am content,* ⟶ *I shall be compelled.*

(*b*) *Accom-* is represented by a joined or disjoined ⟶; thus ⟶ *accommodation,* ⟶ *accommodate.*

134. *Inter-, intro-,* or *enter-* is expressed by ⟶ *nt* joined or disjoined, as may be convenient; thus ⟶ *interfere* ⟶ *interline,* ⟶ *introduce,* ⟶ *introspection,* ⟶ *entertain,* ⟶ *enterprise.*

135. *Magna- magni-* or *magne-,* is expressed by a disjoined ⟶; thus ⟶ *magnanimous,* ⟶ *magnificence,* ⟶ *magnetize.*

136. *Self* is expressed by a disjoined circle *s;* thus ⟶ *self-possessed,* ⟶ *self-defense,* ⟶ *self-conscious.*

137. Before the circled letters ⟶ *in-* is expressed by a small hook written in the *same direction* as the circle; thus ⟶ *inspiration,* ⟶ *instructor,* ⟶ *inscriber,* ⟶ *inhabit.*

PREFIXES.

138. The small hook for *in-* is never used in negative words, that is in words where *in-* has the signification of *not*. In all such cases *in-* must be written with the stroke *n*, as ⌒ *hospitable*, ⌒ *inhospitable*, ⌒ *inhuman*.

139. Negative words which begin with *il-*, *im-*, *in-*, or *un-*, are distinguished from the positive by repeating the first consonant; thus ⌒ *legible*, ⌒ *illegible*; ⌒ *mortal*, ⌒ *immortal*; ⌒ *noxious*, ⌒ *innoxious*; ⌒ *known*, ⌒ *unknown*. Negative words commencing with *ir-* may generally be distinguished without repeating the *r*; thus ⌒ *resolute*, ⌒ *irresolute*. But it is sometimes necessary to repeat the consonant; thus ⌒ *redeemable*, ⌒ *irredeemable*.

Exercise 164.
Read, copy and transcribe.

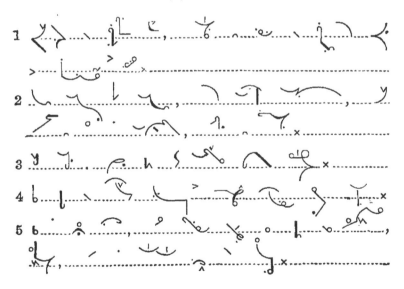

140   COURSE IN ISAAC PITMAN SHORTHAND.

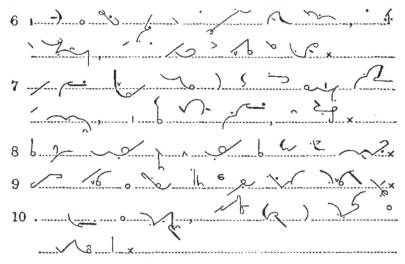

Exercise 165.

Write in Shorthand.

1. *I*-am conscious *that your* misconduct *may* cause considerable confusion.
2. *If-you-can* introduce *a* competent entertainer, *I-will* instruct *the* committee *to* pay *him* well.
3. *In-your* magnificent self-esteem *you* forget-*the* magnitude *of-your* self-imposed task.
4. *If-the* instructor destroys *the* instruments, *he-may* cause irreparable mischief.
5. *I*-am convinced *that-my* interposition *is* necessary *to--remove-the* misconception.
6. *I-shall* contrive *to* be present *at-the* company's *meeting to*-morrow.

CONTRACTIONS.

⌣ *proficient-cy-ly,* ⌣ *deficient-cy-ly,* ⌣ *efficient--cy-ly,* ⌣ *inefficient-cy-ly,* ⌣ *sufficient-cy-iy,* ⌣ *insufficient-cy-ly,* ⌣ *observation,* ⌣ *preservation,* ⌣ *electric,* ⌣ *electrical,* ⌣ *electricity,* ⌣ *inconsiderate,* ⌣ *selfish-ness,* ⌣ *unselfish-ness.*

Exercise 166.

Read, copy, and transcribe.

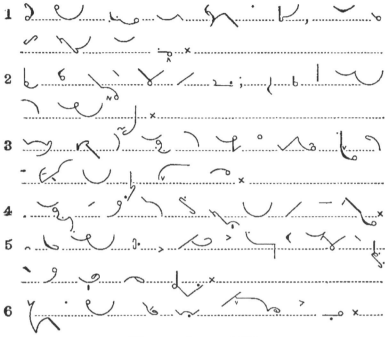

Exercise 167.

Write in Shorthand.

1. We guarantee to-keep a sufficient staff of teachers to-turn out thoroughly efficient stenographers.
2. We-test the efficiency of-every teacher by examination, so-that no inefficient person can find a place.
3. The tests are severe enough to-prove whether a man is proficient or deficient in-his-knowledge.
4. Our proficiency tests are-the result of-long years of observation and trial.
5. We-have-no selfish end in-view, our only object being -the preservation of a high standard in-the-school.
6. You-will-see, therefore, that your conclusions are both inconsistent and inconsiderate, and-we-trust you-will acknowledge-the inconsistency of-your position now that our unselfishness has-been sufficiently proved to-you.

142 COURSE IN ISAAC PITMAN SHORTHAND.

PHRASEOGRAMS.

early consideration, further consideration, further considered, take (taken) into consideration, shall be taken into consideration as soon as convenient, in consequence, and the contrary, on the contrary, to the contrary, at your early convenience, general manager, yours sincerely.

The prefix *con-* may be omitted in any phrase similar to the foregoing.

Exercise 168.

Read, copy, and transcribe.

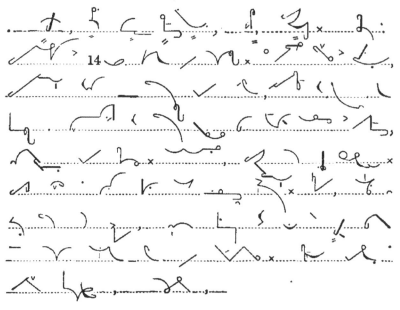

Exercise 169
Write in Shorthand.

The Downes & Plewes Co., *Inc.*,
 Congress St., Brooklyn, *N. Y.*
Gentlemen:

On further-consideration *I-have-*decided *to-*accept *your--*offer *of-the* premises *in* Sycamore Avenue, *subject to* possession *being* given *by-the* 1st September. Perhaps *you-will give* early-consideration *to-the* likelihood *of-this* being arranged, *and* let *me know your* decision *as-soon-as--*convenient. *I-*am-obliged *to* stipulate *for-this* condition *in-*consequence *of-having to* vacate *my* present premises *by-the* date named. *I-must* ask-*you to-*take-into-consideration also *the* fact *that I-shall-be-*obliged *to-*make *several* alterations before-*the* premises *are* exactly suitable *for-my-*requirements. *You* appear *to-think-me* new *to-this* business, whereas, *on-the-*contrary, *I-have-been* engaged *in-it for-the-*last ten *years.* Trusting *to-*receive *a* reply *at-your--early-convenience,*

      *Yours-*sincerely,

LESSON 34.

SUFFIXES AND TERMINATIONS.

140. The suffix -*ing* is generally expressed by the stroke ⌣, and -*ings* by ⌣; thus ⸺ *placing*, ⸺ *facings*, ⸺ *guessing*, ⸺ *meanings;* but when the stroke is not convenient, -*ing* is expressed by a light *dot*, and -*ings* by a light *dash;* thus ⸺ *shipping*, ⸺ *plating*, ⸺ *waving*, ⸺ *winnings*, ⸺ *engravings*.

141. (*a*) The endings -*ality*, -*ility*, -*arity*, etc., are indicated by *disjoining* the stroke preceding the ending; thus ⸺ *finality*, ⸺ *durability*, ⸺ *instability*, ⸺ *popularity*, ⸺ *regularity*, ⸺ *majority*.

(*b*) The termination -*logical-ly* is expressed by a disjoined / *j;* thus ⸺ *mythological*.

142. The suffix -*ment* is expressed by ⌣ *ent*, when the sign ⌢ will not join easily; thus ⸺ *consignment*, ⸺ *commencement*, ⸺ *resentment*, ⸺ *pavement*, ⸺ *refinement;* but ⌢ is written in words like ⸺ *elopement*, ⸺ *commitment*, ⸺ *enjoyment*, ⸺ *agreement*, ⸺ *concealment*, ⸺ *detriment*.

143. The suffix -*mental*, *mentally*, or -*mentality* is expressed by *disjoined* ⌢ *mnt;* thus ⸺ *instrumental--ly-ity*.

144. The suffix -*ly* is generally expressed by ⌒ joined or disjoined, as may be convenient; thus ⸺ *sweetly*, ⸺ *friendly*, ⸺ *absolutely*, ⸺ *confidently*. The *l* hook may sometimes be used

SUFFIXES AND TERMINATIONS.

in words ending in *-ly;* thus ⌇ *briefly,* ⌇ *deeply,* ⌇ *actively.*

145. The suffix *-ship,* is expressed by ⌇ , joined or disjoined, as may be convenient; thus ⌇ *citizenship,* ⌇ *hardship,* ⌇ *clerkship.*

146. The terminations *-fulness, -lessness* and *-lousness* are expressed respectively by *disjoined* ⌇ *fs* and ⌇ *ls,* thus ⌇ *usefulness,* ⌇ *uselessness,* ⌇ *lawfulness,* ⌇ *lawlessness,* ⌇ *sedulousness.*

Exercise 170.
Read, copy, and transcribe.

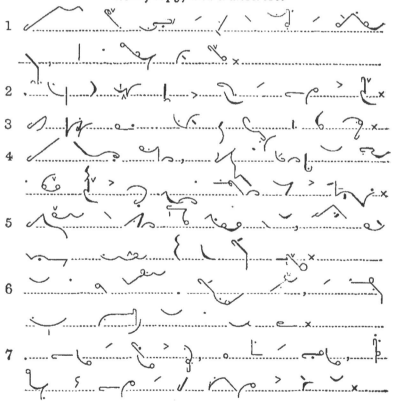

Exercise 171.

Write in Shorthand.

1. Replying *to-your* letter *of-yesterday, we-are* arranging *to-*forward-*the* couplings *and* connecting rods *by--*express *this-*evening.

2. *In-*reply-*to-your-*favor, *we-would* say *that-the-*majority *of-the* designs *are* wanting *in* originality *and* attractability, *and-we-*fear *they-will-not* attain *a* popularity *sufficient to* warrant *us in* stocking *them.*

3. Candidly *speaking, we-think-the* patterns *are* badly designed, *and-though-it-is* distantly possible *that-they-may* sell well, *we-think-we should-be* acting imprudently *if-we* bought *them.*

4. Please-note *that-the-*present order came *through-the* instrumentality *of* Mr.-Smith, *and-is* supplemental *to-the* one we received *yesterday.*

5. *The* delay *of-the* scheme *and-the giv*ing *up of-the first* proposal *was-the* cause *of-great* resentment.

6. *The* inspectorship *of-the* re-arranged district *was-given to-him in* consideration *of-his great* ability.

CONTRACTIONS.

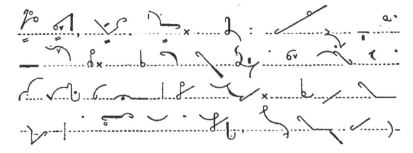

never, nevertheless, notwithstanding, enlarge, enlarged, probable-ly-ility, practice, practise-d, practicable, imperfect-ion, satisfaction, satisfactory, unsatisfactory.

Exercise 172.
Read, copy, and transcribe.

SUFFIXES AND TERMINATIONS. 147

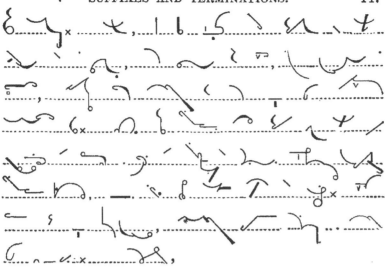

Exercise 173.
Write in Shorthand.

Mr. George Manning,
   St. Paul, Minn.
Dear-Sir:

   In-reply-*to-your*-favor *of-yesterday we would*-say *that--we-never* hesitate *to*-replace *a* machine *which does-not give* complete *satisfaction.* Nevertheless, where *practicable we*-like *to* assure *ourselves that-the-imperfection was* present *when-the*-machine left *our hands.* As *a* rule, *this-is very improbable, because-we*-take *every care to* insure *an* absence *of imperfection in every* machine *sent-out.* We-are-satisfied, however, that in-the-present-instance, *notwithstanding our care, there-has-been an* oversight, *probably on-the*-part *of one of-the* new *hands* engaged since-*we enlarged our* works, *and-we-shall-be*-glad *if-you-will* return-*the unsatisfactory* machine *at-our* cost. *It-is* practically *impossible that*-such *an* error *should-be* committed again. *It-is satisfactory to us to know that-you-will-not* permit *this* accident *to* interfere *with your* friendship *for our* firm. We flatter *ourselves that-you*-recognize *us as* practical men, *who-have always practised* straightforward business methods.
                              Respectfully-yours,

PHRASEOGRAMS.

I have concluded, satisfactory conclusion, unsatisfactory conclusion, under the circumstances, best of my ability, best of our ability, best of your ability, best of their ability.

Exercise 174.
Read, copy, and transcribe.

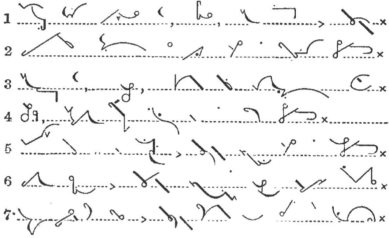

Exercise 175.
Write in Shorthand.

1. *I*-am confident *that under-the-circumstances you-will* reconsider *your* decision, *and-will* accept-*the* consignment.

2. *Having* considered *all-the* circumstances, *I-have*-concluded *to-give you-the* agency, *and-I*-hope-*you-will* exert *yourself to-the* best-*of-your*-ability *to*-make-*it* profitable *to* both *of us.*

3. *We*-regret *to*-report *that-the* negotiations *have come to an unsatisfactory*-conclusion.

4. *We*-assure-*you that-the* business *shall-be* looked after *to-the* best-*of-our*-ability, *and-that-we-shall* spare *no* pains *to-bring-the-*matter *to a satisfactory*-conclusion.

LESSON 35.

OMISSION OF CONSONANTS.

147. In order to obtain more facile outlines, certain medial consonants may be omitted, as follows:

(a) *P* between *m* and *t*, or between *m* and *sh;* thus ⌒ *prompt,* ⌒ *stamped,* ⌒ *redemption,* ⌒ *presumption.*

(b) *T* between the circle *s* and another consonant; thus ⌒ *postage,* ⌒ *postage stamp,* ⌒ *postpone,* ⌒ *testimony.*

(c) *K* or *g* between *ng* and *t* or *sh;* thus ⌒ *adjunct,* ⌒ *conjunction,* ⌒ *anxious,* ⌒ *sanction.*

Exercise 176.

Read, copy, and transcribe.

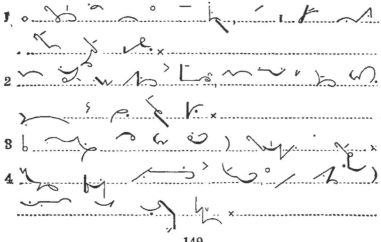

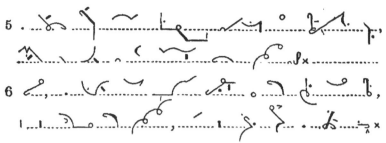

Exercise 177.
Write in Shorthand.

Mr. Charles Warner,
  Cleveland, Ohio.
Dear-Sir:

Your-favor of-the 4th is at hand. We-consider Barnes' offer almost a presumption. At-any-rate, it-is-no temptation to us to-sell, and-we-have promptly declined it. Please use the strongest efforts to secure Anderson's order. You-can promise punctual delivery in a week's-time. The market here is very restless, and business is languishing in-consequence. We-note your remarks about-the sacks, and-will attend to-the-matter immediately.

                                Yours-truly,

CONTRACTIONS.

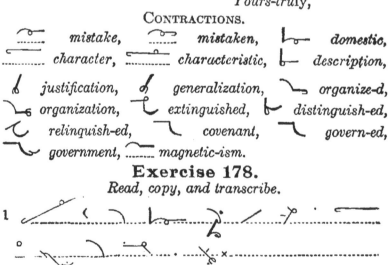

Exercise 178.
Read, copy, and transcribe.

OMISSION OF CONSONANTS. 151

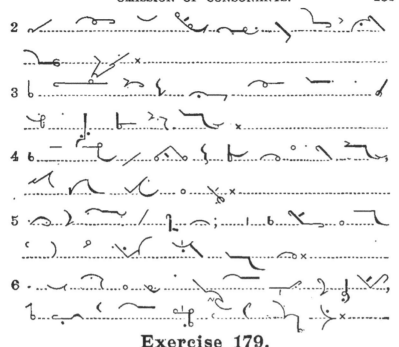

Exercise 179.
Write in Shorthand.

1. *We-regret-the mistake in* forwarding *you a description of-the* wrong cloth, *and-we-have* despatched *a special messenger with-the* correct details.
2. *We* read *in-the* new *magazine that-the-government has relinquished-the* claim *to* control *the domestic* policy *of-the* ruler *and-there-is justification for-it.*
3. *The distinguished* speaker *in-his generalization* summed *up-the character of-the organization with characteristic* ability, *though-we-think he-was mistaken in-his* condemnation *of-the* recently signed *covenant.*
4. *We-have organized a* new system *of-*collection *which--we* hope *will* reduce, *if-it-does-not* entirely *extinguish, the* losses *on* returns.
5. *A magnet is a* body *which-has-the* property *of* attracting iron *and other magnetic* bodies.
6. *The* science *of magnetism has-been* studied *for-*many centuries.

COURSE IN ISAAC PITMAN SHORTHAND.

PHRASEOGRAMS.

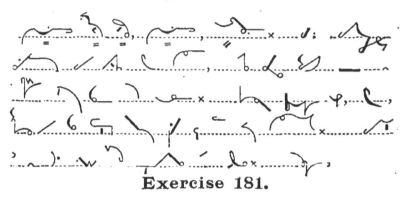

Exercise 180.

Read, copy, and transcribe.

Exercise 181.

Write in Shorthand.

Mr. S. Webb,
    New Orleans, La.

Dear-Sir:

We-have-just-received *a* cable *informing us that-the-*goods *you-*wrote about last-week *have-been* shipped *and may-be expected* here *at-the-*end *of next-*week. Last-month's sales, *it-*appears, were *unusually* heavy, *and-there--was a* little delay *in* obtaining exactly *the* material required. *Our* correspondents *inform us* also *that-it-is* just-possible *that-*prices *will* rise, *and-that* instructions *must-be-sent immediately if-they-are to-*forward *a* further supply *at-*present rates.

                     Yours-truly,

LESSON 36.

FIGURES.

148. Figures *one* to *seven*, and the figure *nine* are written in shorthand. All other numbers, except round numbers, are represented by the ordinary Arabic numerals. Round numbers, dollars, and pounds, may be expressed by using the shorthand letters, as follows:

⌣ for *hundred* or *hundredth;* thus 4⌣ , 400.

(for *thousand;* thus 5(, 5,000; 5⌐ , 500,000; 250(, $250,000.

⌒ for *million;* thus 4⌒ , 4,000,000; 4⌒ , 400,000,000.

╲ for *billion;* thus 2╲ , two *billions.*

Dollars and *cents* may be written thus 7¹⁶, $7.16.

Exercise 182.
Write in Shorthand.

The Shah *of* Persia *owns a* pearl *which-is* valued *at* $650,000, *and-the* Pope *is* said *to-be-the* possessor *of-one* worth $80,000. Queen Victoria *had a* necklace *of* pink pearls *which-was* worth $80,000; *but-the* ladies *of-the* Rothschild family possess pearls *of* far *greater* value. Baroness Rothschild *has a* pearl necklace valued *at* $200,000.

The cotton marketed since September 1 exceeds 12¼ million bales. *The* actual *production cannot have-been* far *short of* 14,000,000 bales. Spinners' takings *from* September 1 *to* June 2 amounted *to* 10,269,000, *of-which* 2,514,000 were British, 3,815,000 Continental, etc., *and* 3,940,000 American *and* Canadian. *It-is* computed *that- -the*-present supply, visible *and* invisible, amounts *to*

6,768,000 bales. *The prospects for next year* appear *to be any*where between 11,000,000 *and* 14,000,000 bales, *but it-is-impossible to* predict *more* closely than *this.*

We-have-your check *for* $115.25, *which-we-have-*placed *to-your-*credit. Please-note-*that* since-*we* last wrote-*you* the price *of* steel *has*' advanced $1.25 per ton. *Our* price per gross *of* sharpeners *is-*now $18, f. o. b. New Orleans *or* Boston.

Exercise 183.

Write in Shorthand.

Mr. C. N. Pitt,
    Louisville, Ky.

*Dear-*Sir:

*We should-be-*pleased *to-*purchase *the* return *or over* issue copies *of-your* magazine *and* pamphlet *publication as* waste-paper. *We-*send men *to* bag *it up and* take-*it* away *and-we* pay prompt cash. *We* also guarantee *that- -each and every* copy received *shall go to-our* paper mill *and- -be* destroyed.

If printed *on* rag paper *we-will* pay *you* 60 cents per 100 lbs. *When you have an* accumulation *of* 1,000 lbs. *or over, if-you-will* advise *us by* telephone *or* mail, *we-will- -be-*pleased *to-*send *for it.*

This quotation *is subject to* change *without* notice.

                                   Very-truly-yours,

Exercise 184.

Write in Shorthand.

Mr. S. A. Walker,
    Minneapolis, Minn.

*Dear-*Sir:

*We-*enclose *our* check *for* $7.50 *which-will-be* accepted *in* part payment *of any* suit *or overcoat* purchased *at-our* wardrobes, 290 *or* 314 Main Street, before September 25th.

FIGURES. 155

At-this season *of-the* year *to* dispose *of-our* surplus stock *and-as* an additional inducement *to-you* *to-*test *the* convenience *and-character of* "Semi-ready" tailoring—*we-*make *this* sincere *and* genuine offer.

"Semi-ready" means suits ready *to-*try *on*, finished *to* order, *no* ugly misfits, *no* delays. *Our* system *is-not an* experiment, *as-in* five *years we-have* established *and--*now operate twenty-nine wardrobes *in-the United States and* Canada.

*All-*prices *are* woven *in-the* inside breast pocket. Suits $20 *to* $40. Money back *if* dissatisfied.

Respectfully,

CONTRACTIONS.

captain, capable, incapable, appointment, disappointment, attainment or atonement, entertainment, contentment, indignant-ation, resignation, antagonist-ic-ism, inscribe-d, inscription, instructive, instruction.

Exercise 185.

Read, copy, and transcribe.

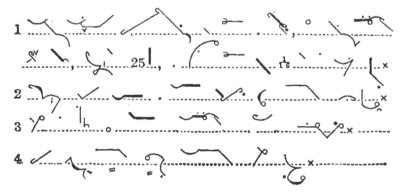

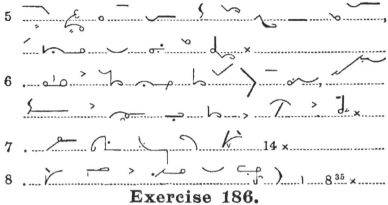

Exercise 186.

Write in Shorthand.

1. *We-believe-that* Captain Walker *has* declined *to inscribe his* name *on-the* register *of-members of-the* club.
2. *The* resignation *of so* capable *a* man *has been a great-* *-disappointment to-the-members.*
3. *I-*understand *he-is* indignant *at-the* treatment *given to-his* late *antagonist.*
4. *He-thinks-the* committee *are* incapable *of-*making sufficient atonement *for-their* conduct.
5. *His* example *may-be* followed *by-others, so-that I-*fear*--the* proposed *entertainment will-be impossible* now.
6. *This* period *of* inactivity *is quite* unexampled *in-the* -history *of-the* company.
7. *The* appointment *of Mr.* Black *as* assistant *general-* manager *may* alter *the* present state *of things, and* possibly produce *contentment in-the-*minds *of-the* shareholders.
8. *It-may-be-that-the* amount *you-*mentioned *was* $25.50, *or a* little *over.*

Phraseograms.

⸺ *in regard to,* ⸺ *with regard to,* ⸺ *having regard to,* ⸺ *with respect to,* ⸺ *with relation to,* ⸺ *in relation to,* ⸺ *with reference to,* ⸺ *I have received.*

FIGURES. 157

Exercise 187.

Read, copy, and transcribe.

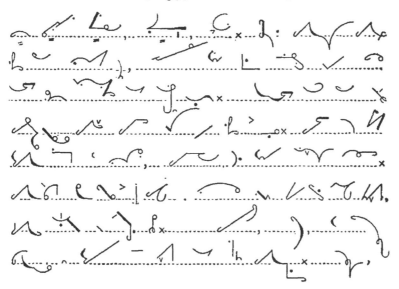

Exercise 188.

Write in Shorthand.

Mr. W. C. Shaw,
  Memphis, Tenn.
Dear-Sir:

In-reply-*to-your* inquiry *with*-regard-*to our special* grade index cards, *we*-enclose-herewith *several* samples *with* prices marked *on* each. *Having*-regard-*to-the* fact *that-you-are* likely *to*-take *large* quantities, *we-have*--quoted-*you very*-low-prices. *With*-reference-*to your observations as-to-the* extension *of-the* system, *we-may*-say *that-we-have*-received letters *from all* parts *of-the* country assuring *us that-it gives the* utmost *satisfaction. We-shall--be*-glad *to*-hear further *from-you in*-relation-*to-the* typewriter supplies *for-which-we*-quoted-*you* last week.

Respectfully-yours,

LESSON 37.
COMPOUND WORDS.

149. Compounds of *here, there, where,* etc., are written as follows.

hereat, hereto, hereof, herewith, heretofore, herein, hereon, thereat, thereto, therewith, therein, thereon, whereat, whereto, whereof, wherewith, wherein, whereon, whereas, whereabout, inasmuch, furthermore.

Exercise 189.
Read, copy, and transcribe.

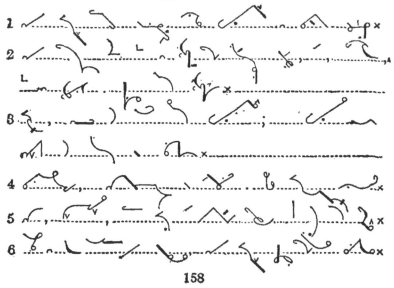

Exercise 190.

Write in Shorthand.

1. *We*-enclose-here*with-the* specimens whereof *we* spoke, *and* whereto *we* ask *your* attention.
2. *The* documents whereon *we* rely, *and* wherein *you-will-* *-*find *our* case fully stated, *are* enclosed-herewith.
3. *The* facts *of-the* case were laid before*-him* last Christmas or thereabouts, whereat *he-was surprised, and* whereon *he* expressed *his* views *in-the*-letter herein enclosed.
4. *We-have-your*-letter *of-the first-instant, and-the* accounts therein referred *to are* enclosed-herewith.
5. *We-call your* attention thereto, *and* entrust *the* consideration thereof *to*-yourself *and* partner.
6. *I* questioned *the information* whereof *he* spoke, *and-I-sent him your*-letters, pointing*-out that-therein he-would* find*-the true* statement *of-the* case.
7. Hereat *he-was, it-*seems delighted, *and* hereto *he*-drew*-the* attention *of-the members,* whereat *they-*were-pleased, *and* where*upon they* withdrew *their* opposition.
8. Please-note*-that-the-*goods named *in-the-*order enclosed-herewith *must-be delivered* forthwith.

Exercise 191.

Write in Shorthand.

Mr. Abraham Samuels,
   St. Louis, Mo.
*Dear-*Sir:

Will-you let-us give you information wherewith *you-* *-can* save *from* twenty *to* fifty per-cent. *in-your* Billing *and* Order Department? *The information* offered herewith *is yours for-the* asking. See slip attached here*to.* *Would thank-you for an acknowledgment.*

   Yours-very-truly,

Exercise 192.
Write in Shorthand.

Mr. Benjamin J. Neale,
   St. Joseph, Mo.
Dear-Sir:
   Herewith *we have-the-pleasure to* enclose *our* new price-list, wherein *you-will*-find *particulars of-several* lines *that should* appeal *to-you. You-will-see-the* details whereof *we speak on* page 44. *Respectfully-yours,*

CONTRACTIONS.

discharge-d, displeasure, dissimilar, expenditure, expensive, extraordinary, extravagant - ce, manufacture- d, manufacturer, intelligent, intelligence, intelligible, advertise-d-ment.

Exercise 193.
Read, copy, and transcribe.

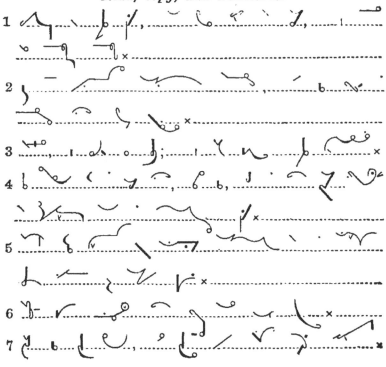

Exercise 194.
Write in Shorthand.

Mr. Charles Sellers,
 Detroit, Mich.
Dear-Sir:

 After *an extraordinary expenditure of*-time *and* money, *we-have*-succeeded *in manufactur*ing *an* article, *which-will*-prevent-*the* extravagant waste *of* starch *which--*now *goes on in-our public and* private laundries. *The* article *is* entirely *dissimilar to anything* hitherto invented. *It-is-not-expensive, and-we-believe it-will-be largely* taken-*up by manufacturers,* dyers, *and* finishers, *immediately it-is put on-the* market. *We-want an intelligent* man *to-represent us at-the* approaching Exhibition; *a* man *of*-quick *intelligence, able to* explain *intelligibly the* merits *of-the* new invention, *and who-would* discharge *in-the* best possible-*way the* duties *of-our* agent *on-the*-spot. *We-under*stand *that-you would-be* willing *to*-consider *an* offer *of*-such an *appointment, and-we should-be*-glad *to-have-you call-upon-us* some day *next*-week *to* discuss-*the*-matter. *With-regard-to* your complaint about-*the* borax, *we-think-you had* cause *for-your displeasure, and-we-will-see-the manufacturer.*

       Respectfully-yours,

Exercise 195.
Write in Shorthand.

Mr. Clement Newton,
 Dayton, Ohio.
Dear-Sir:

 May-we advise *you to-try-the expenditure of a* few dollars *on an* advertisement *in-our* columns? *You-will--find-the* cost *not extravagant, while-the* result, *we-are* confident, *will-be very satisfactory. We-know-the* old ways *of* displaying *advertisements, and-we* adopt entirely *different* methods, less *expensive, and* far *more* effective. *We*-enclose *our* rates *and-trust-to-*hear *from-you.*

       Yours-truly,

LESSON 38.
INTERSECTIONS.

150. The shorthand writer may provide himself with brief, distinctive, and easily written outlines for the titles of companies, officials, etc., and for frequent colloquial phrases, by employing the principle of intersection, or the writing of one stroke consonant through another, as in the examples which follow, and from which the student may devise similar phraseograms to suit his requirements. Thus ＼ may be used for *party;* ＼ for *bank;* | for *attention;* | for *department;* ／ for *Journal;* ＿ for *company;* (for *authority;*) for *society;* ／ for *railroad;* ＼ for *arrange-d-ment;* etc.; as ⟋ *political party,* ⟋ *party, question,* ⟋ *Bank of New York,* ⟋ *National Bank,* ⟋ *my attention has been called,* ⟋ *I ask attention,* ⟋ *wagon department,* ⟋ *shipping department,* ⟋ *Pitman's Journal,* ⟋ *Journal of Commerce,* ⟋ *Hazel & Co.,* ⟋ *The Jones Publishing Co.,* ⟋ *local authority,* ⟋ *medical authorities,* ⟋ *dramatic society,* ⟋ *Pennsylvania R.R.,* ⟋ *South Carolina R.R.,* ⟋ *I shall arrange,* ⟋ *I have arranged,* ⟋ *please make arrangements.* When the direction of the letters will not allow of intersection, the second stroke may be written close to or under the first; as ⟋ *Knox & Co.*

INTERSECTIONS.

Exercise 196.

Write in Shorthand.

1. *The* party leaders *are to-*meet *to-*morrow-evening *to--*make arrangements *for-the coming* election.
2. *The* manager *of-the* State Bank writes *to-the* "Engineering Journal," *calling* attention *to-the* new savings department.
3. *The New York Publishing* Co. *has* issued *a* new catalog *of-its* works.
4. *The* medical authorities declare *the* port absolutely free *from-the* plague.
5. *The* Baltimore Musical *and* Dramatic Society *gives its first entertainment of-the* season *to-*morrow-evening.
6. *A* big increase *is* reported *in-the* traffic returns *of-the* Missouri Pacific Railway.
7. *I-will* arrange*-the* matter *as I-have* arranged *it* before.

CONTRACTIONS.

individual, investment, interest, interested, uninteresting, disinterested-ness, applicable-ility, astonish-ed-ment, certificate, contingency.

Exercise 197.

Write in Shorthand.

Mr. R. Mason,
    Toronto, Can.
*Dear-*Sir:

Referring *to-the individual who called* last-week respecting an *investment, it-may interest-you to know that-we-have* discovered, *to-our astonishment, that-the-*man *has* since left*-the* country. *We-were-told by a* perfectly *disinterested* person *that-the stranger had had a* far *from uninteresting* career. *He* won *a high*-speed *certificate when-he-was* sixteen *years* old, *and when-his* father died *was* left *with sufficient* funds *to*-meet *any* ordinary *contingency. He* lost *much* money, *however, and* seems *to-have* intended *to*-make *a* safe *investment of-the* remainder. *We*-now *see-the applicability of-his* remark about *not having* "*all-your* eggs *in-one* basket," *though-we-could--not* make-*it applicable to-his* business *at-the*-time. *We--will* let *you know if-we* hear *anything*-further about-*him.*

Respectfully-yours,

Exercise 198.
Write in Shorthand.

Mr. George Hewson,
    Cumberland, Md.
Dear-Sir:

We-desire *to-call your*-attention *to-the* fact *that-this--is-the-most* appropriate time *for* placing contracts *for* advertisements. *Knowing that-you-are-interested in-this--matter, we-take-the-liberty of* enclosing *a* pamphlet explaining *our* latest methods *of* distributing circulars, etc., *and-we*-hope-*you-may-be* inclined *to put our* methods *to-the* test. *We-have a* staff *large* enough *to*-meet *any contingency.*

Yours-very-truly,

Exercise 199.
Write in Shorthand.

Mr. James Lee,
    Richmond, Va.
Dear-Sir:

We-are astonished to-learn *that your certificate has--not-yet* reached *you, and-we-are* making inquiry *of-the* framer. *He-is* usually *a very* prompt *individual, and--we-can* scarcely *think-he-has neglected our instructions.*

Respectfully-yours,

LESSON 39.
DISTINGUISHING VOWELS.

151. Regular and systematic practice in the writing and reading of shorthand characters, with a careful following of the rules for the indication of vowels, will enable the student to dispense with vocalization to a large extent. Nevertheless, he should not hesitate to insert a vowel where it seems necessary for the sake of distinction, as, for instance, in such words as ⌒ *lady* (to distinguish it from *load*), ⌒ *enemy* (to distinguish from *name*), ⌐ *extricate* (to distinguish from *extract*). An uncommon proper name, too, should always be vocalized when written for the first time, though the outline may be left unvocalized should the name occur again in the same matter. Speaking generally, the stenographer should rather err on the side of over-vocalization than run any risk of illegibility by omitting necessary vowels.

Exercise 200.

In this exercise the italic letters indicate the vowels which should be inserted.

We should-neither *a*ccept any theories nor adopt any views, however v*o*luble the *a*dvocates of-such-may-be except we-are convinced that-they-are authorized, and--have-been tested and *a*ttested by-those upon whose veracity we-can rely, or unless our-own reason approve*s* of-them and-we-have *a*mple proof that-though they-may--have some defects, their adoption will-be valuable to us in-the-main, that-we-may employ them to-the benefit of--ourselves and others, and-that-they-will-be readily available on occasions of necessity. No matter how *a*pposite the arguments may appear which-are *a*dduced to-move us from an *o*pposite opinion, we should-be as *a*damant in the face of any demand upon-the feelings, which-our reason does-not sanction. Thus, any *a*ttempt to-tempt us to foolish actions will-only *e*nd in-the failure *of-the* tempter. We-have-been end*ow*ed with mental faculties far-and-*a*way above those with-which-the lower *a*nimals are end*ue*d, in order that-we-may protect ourselves from-our enem*i*es, and may add to-our happiness. It-is a fact, however, that-such-is-the *e*ffect of-persuasion upon some persons of weak will that-they become as mere wax in-the hands of-those-who-would lure them to--ruin. With-such people it-seems only necessary for a fluent rogue to *a*dvance an *a*lluring prospect of an *a*ffluent position at-little cost, and-they fall at-once, without a defence, into-the trap set for-them. Is-not-this-the secret of almost every-successful fraud we-have-heard or read of in-any-nation? There-are, *a*las, too-many--persons who-make-it their vocation or *a*vocation in life to dupe others less able than themselves. They-have no feelings of honor, or *e*lse would-not prey on-the failings of-those around. They despise veracity, and-their greed for gold amounts almost to voracity. To obtain possession of-riches they-make light of-every opposition, and are slow to *a*dmit themselves beaten. They-are *a*verse to honest labor, and-yet they spare no pains to become versed in-the cunning arts necessary to-extract money from their victims, and to-extricate themselves from-the consequences of-their illegal actions. They devise a plot, and, under-the semblance of *a*dvice, they *o*perate on-the greed and-credulity of ignorant persons, and--having thrown them off their guard, lead them into foolish *a*dventures. Truly "A fool and-his money are easily parted." We should-not *a*ttach too-much importance to a scheme because-it-is introduced with a flourish of fair words, nor should-we touch any speculative *a*ffair without first subjecting it to an accurate examination. If-we-could only examine the *a*nnual returns of failures and *a*nalyze their-causes, we should-find that many are attributable to an *u*tter absence of-judgment in-the conduct of business, and an over confidence in-the n*i*cety and honesty of-others.

CONTRACTIONS.

demonstrate,   remonstrate,   ministry,
familiar-ity, preliminary,   singular,
indispensable-y.

Exercise 201.

Write in Shorthand.

1. *I-think-the* railroad company's *representative was--much* too *familiar*, and *I-shall remonstrate with* him *on-the* first opportunity.
2. *It-is singular that-they should* choose such *a* time *to demonstrate* their strength.
3. *It-was* originally *his* intention *to*-join *the ministry*, but *he-was* obliged *to* abandon *the* idea.
4. *The* original owner *was a very singular individual*, *who never* indulged *in familiarity with anyone*.
5. *An indispensable preliminary was-the* signing *of-the* register *at-the* door *of-the* hall.
6. *It-is indispensably* necessary *that-you-should-be*-present *at-the* meeting *to*-morrow.

Exercise 202.

Write in Shorthand.

Mr. Richard Young,
 Milwaukee, Wis.
*Dear-*Sir:

Replying *to-your*-favor *of-the* 1st *inst., the* original *of-the* document *to-which-you*-refer *may-be*-seen here, after *a preliminary* examination *of-your* credentials. *This-is an indispensable* condition, *and-it-is singular that-you-should-not-be familiar with-it. The circumstance would* appear *to* show *that-you-are a* stranger *in-this* district. *We should-be*-pleased, however, *to see-you* whenever *you* care *to-*call.

Yours-truly,

LESSON 40.

DISTINGUISHING OUTLINES.

152. There are some words which have *outlines of their own;* that is, they are readily recognized by their distinctive forms, which it is difficult to read for any but the words they are intended to represent. The following are examples of such words: *instincts, disqualifies, distinction, pronounce, miserably, fortunately.*

153. The following list of similar words, distinguished by a difference of outline, is selected from the longer list given in "Pitman's Shorthand Instructor."

petrify, putrefy; passionate, patient; purpose, propose, perhaps; appropriate, property, propriety, purport; appropriation, preparation; proffer, prefer; provide, pervade; prosecute, persecute, prosecution, persecution; detriment-al, determined; debtor, editor; defray, defer; courage, carriage; factor, factory; favored, favorite; staid, steady, considerate, considered; impassioned, impatient; unavoidable, inevitable; learned (verb), learned (adjective); regard, regret. Pure and poor, and derivatives of these words, are written in the third position, and are distinguished thus: *pure, purely*, *pureness*; *poor*, *poorly*, *poorness*.

Exercise 203.

Write in Shorthand. The distinguishing words are printed in SMALL CAPITALS.

1. *A* man *of-his* DISTINCTION *in* learning *can* easily say *whether-the thing will* PUTREFY *or* PETRIFY.
2. *The* PASSIONATE behavior *of-the* MISERABLE fellow contrasted strongly *with-the* PATIENT bearing *of-his* companion.
3. PERHAPS *you* PROPOSE *to* accomplish *your* PURPOSE *in*-another-*way*.
4. *We*-consider *it very* APPROPRIATE *that-the*-PROPERTY should go to a man *of*-such PROPRIETY.
5. *What-is-the* PURPORT *of-the* APPROPRIATION *for-which--you-are* making such careful PREPARATION?
6. *If-you* PREFER *to*-PROFFER *your* services free *of*-charge, *I-shall* DEFER *my*-proposal *to*-DEFRAY *your* expenses.
7. *The* presence *of-the* ladies *will*-PROVIDE *an* air *of--quietness that-is* sure *to*-PERVADE-*the* whole conference.
8. *I*-fear-*the* PROSECUTION *has* become *a* PERSECUTION, *and-that-they* PROSECUTE *the* case now *rather to* PERSECUTE *the* UNFORTUNATE man than *to*-secure justice.
9. *The* POORNESS *of-the* bread *was* compensated *by--the* PURENESS *of-the* milk.
10. *I*-REGARD-*the* EDITOR *as-my* DEBTOR *for-the*-amount, but *I*-REGRET *to* say he does-not recognize *my*-claim.
11. *The* STEADY COURAGE *of-the* STAID student *in* stopping *the* CARRIAGE won-*the* admiration *of-the* FACTOR, *and-the* youth *is*-now engaged *at-the* FACTORY.
12. *We*-were-FAVORED *with an* IMPASSIONED address *from our* FAVORITE speaker, *who*, IMPATIENT *at what-he* CONSIDERED-*the* want-*of* CONSIDERATE treatment *by-the* mayor, gave *us a* rousing discourse.

13. *It-was* INEVITABLE, *in-the* UNAVOIDABLE absence *of* Mr. Brown, *that-you-should* RESUME *your* position *and* REASSUME *the* control *of-the* FACTORY.

14. FORTUNATELY, *his* INSTINCT *as a* scholar led *him to--PRONOUNCE-the* words properly, *or he-would-have--been* DISQUALIFIED.

CONTRACTIONS.

indescribable, *indiscriminate,* *sensible-ility,* *peculiar-ity,* *perpendicular,* *proportion-ed,* *proportionate-ly,* *establish-ed-ment.*

Exercise 204.

Write in Shorthand.

(a) *Dear-*Sir: The *peculiar* novelty about *which-you* inquire *is* simply *indescribable in a* letter, *as we-are* perpetually *informing* inquirers. *We-have-*just *established a* branch *in New York,* where *you-can inspect-the* article *at any-*time. *Respectfully-yours,*

(b) *Dear-*Sir: The *indiscriminate* attacks *which-you have-been* pleased *to-*make *upon-the* management *of-this establishment are* altogether *out-of proportion to-the* gravity *of-the mistake we* made, *and-we* appeal *to-you to* discontinue them *at-*once. *Respectfully-yours,*

(c) *Dear-*Sir: Replying-*to-your-*letter *of-yesterday, we--*think *your-*writing *is too perpendicular, and-that-you do--not* observe *a* due *proportion in-the-*size *of-the* letters. *Your* downstrokes *are by-no-*means *proportionate in* length *to-the* horizontals, *and you-are* rather *indiscriminate in-the* use *of-*phrases. The most *sensible* plan *for a* man *of--your sensibility would-be to-*take *a* course *of-*private lessons, *and-we-shall-be-*pleased *to* see-*you with a* view *to-this. We-do-not* propose *to establish a* branch *in-your* town *at--*present. *Yours-respectfully,*

The following letter to be written in Shorthand.

Exercise 205.

Messrs. L. Baring & Co.,
    Indianapolis, Ind.
Gentlemen:

    *We-are-*deeply *sensible of-your-*kindness *in giving us--the information* set forth *in-your-*favor *of-the* 10th *inst., and-we-shall-be-*pleased *to-*reciprocate *at any-*time *when--it-may-be in-our* power *to-do-so.* The business *is a peculiar one, and-we-have to be* careful *not to-*take *an* undue *proportion of-*risk *by indiscriminate* haste. *Thanking you* again *for-your* courtesy, *we* remain,

                      Yours-very-truly,

Exercise 206.

Mr. G. E. Heeney,
    Savannah, Ga.
*Dear-*Sir:

    *We-have-your-*letter *of-yesterday, and-we-are* looking into-*the-*matter. *We-are quite* unable *at-*present *to-*explain-*the* cause *of-the* trouble *with-the* last consignment, *but-we-will* write-*you* again *in* a day *or-two.*

                      Yours-truly,

Exercise 207.

Messrs. Stainer & Co.,
    Boston, Mass.
Gentlemen·

    *We-are-much-*obliged *for-your information* about-*the* stain, *and-we-*enclose-herewith trial order *for* five gallons *of No.* 3 quality, dark. *We-shall-be-*glad *if-you-will* also send a specimen *of-the* work *of-No.* 5a.

                      Yours-truly,

Exercise 208.

Mr. H. A. Carey,
    Washington, D. C.
*Dear-*Sir:

    *We-*take-*pleasure in-*enclosing-*you* a card herewith, *upon* presentation *of-which at our* Mineral Spring

Pavilion, *we-will-be*-pleased *to*-serve *you with any of-our* artificial mineral waters *in-which-you-may-be particularly interested, and-will give you any-information you-may* desire.

Our waters *are* compounded *according-to-the* standard analysis *of-the* various *natural* springs, *and are manufactured* only *with* chemically pure salts *and* distilled water.

We-feel *that-the* fact *that our* waters *are* prescribed *by, and* used *in-the* families *of-over* eighteen hundred physicians *in-this* state, *should-be a sufficient* guaranty *of-their* purity *and* wholesomeness.

This pavilion *was* erected *in* 1904 *at-the* request *of* numerous physicians, *and-is* used *during-the* early morning *hours by* patients *who-have-been sent there by-their* physicians *to-take one of-the* various cures, *and* derive, *at-the--same-time, the* benefit *of* exercise *in-the* open air.

Yours-respectfully,

Exercise 209.

Mr. C. Singer,
  New York, N. Y.
Dear-Sir:

The Department *of* Education, Corner Park Avenue & 59th Street, Borough *of* Manhattan (where specifications *may-be* obtained), invites bids until 3 p. m., Sept. 14th, 1915, *for* furnishing *and delivering* text-books, maps, globes, charts, pictures, etc., *for-the* Day *and*-Evening Elementary Schools, *the* Day *and*-Evening High-Schools, *and-the* Training-Schools *of-the* City *of New York.*

We-will-be-pleased *to* arrange *for-the* execution *of* Bid Bond required.

Yours-very-truly,

THE GRAMMALOGS AND CONTRACTIONS.

Arranged in the order in which they are given in the preceding pages.

LESSON 1. ⎯ a *or* an, . the, ⎯ all, too *or* two, ⎯ of, to, ⎯ owe *or* Oh! he, ⎯ on, but.

LESSON 2. ⎯ awe *or* ought, who, ⎯ (*up*) and, (*up*) should, ⎯ happy, up, ⎯ put, ⎯ by, buy or bye, be, ⎯ to be, at, it, ⎯ out.

LESSON 3. ⎯ had, do, ⎯ different-ce, ⎯ much, which, ⎯ each, large, ⎯ can, ⎯ come, ⎯ go *or* ago, ⎯ give-n.

LESSON 4. ⎯ half, if, have, ⎯ thanked, think, ⎯ youth, ⎯ though, them *or* they.

LESSON 5. ⎯ I *or* eye, how, ⎯ why, ay (*yes*), ⎯ beyond, you, ⎯ with, when, ⎯ what, would.

LESSON 6. ⎯ saw, so *or* us, ⎯ see, was, ⎯ whose, shall, ⎯ wish, usual-ly.

LESSON 7. ⎯ as *or* has, is *or* his, ⎯ because, ⎯ itself, ⎯ those, this, ⎯ these *or* thus, ⎯ me *or* my, him *or* may, ⎯ myself, himself, are, ⎯ our *or* hour.

LESSON 8. first, ⎯ most, must, ⎯ influence, ⎯ influenced, next, ⎯ in *or* any, no *or* know, ⎯ own, ⎯ suggest-ed.

LESSON 9. as his, is as, this is or themselves, ourselves, special-ly, speak, several, yes, high, house, we, way.

LESSON 10. language or owing, thing, young, anything, nothing, something, or, your, year.

LESSON 12. apply, people, by all, able, belief or believed, at all, tell, till, deliver-ed-y, call, equal-ly, doctor, Dr., dear, during, dollar-s.

LESSON 13. for, over, ever-y, valuation, evil, other, more or remark-ed, remarkable-y, mere or Mr., nor, near, initial-ed-ly.

LESSON 14. from, very, however, they are, their or there, through or threw, therefore, principle or principal-ly, liberty, member or remember-ed, number-ed.

LESSON 15. strength, try, truth, true, chair, cheer, larger, journal, children, largely, care, sure, pleasure, surprise, surprised.

LESSON 16. happen, upon, been, had been, done, down, general-ly, often, Phonography, phonographer, phonographic, have been, within, southern, northern.

GRAMMALOGS AND CONTRACTIONS.

LESSON 17. approve, behalf, above, out of, advantage, difficult, difficulty, which have, suggestion, suggestive, one, opinion, altogether, together, insurance.

LESSON 19. architect-ure-al, neglect-ed, prospect, object-ed, subject-ed, expect-ed, unexpected-ly, respect-ed, suspect-ed, inspect-ed-tion.

LESSON 20. signify-ied-ficant, significance, signification, insignificant, insignificance, subscribe-d, subscription, balance, balances, balanced, deliverance, knowledge, acknowledge.

LESSON 21. will, while, important-ce, improve-d-ment, impossible, improves-ments, whether, unquestionable-y, yesterday, January, February, November, United States.

LESSON 22. perspective, prospective, productive, obstructive, objective, subjective, destructive, respective, irrespective, retrospective, respectively, defective, executive.

LESSON 23. abstraction, obstruction, subjection, objection, destruction, uniform-ity-ly, unanimity-ous.

LESSON 24. ⌃ Revd., ⌢ regular, ⌍ irregular, ⌍ public-sh-ed, ⌍ publication, ⌃ republic, ⌃ republican, ⌃ repugnant-ce, ⌃ represent-ed, ⌃ representation, ⌃ representative, ⌃ responsible-ity, ⌍ irresponsible-ity.

LESSON 26. ⎯ quite, _ could, ⎯ according, according to, or cart, ⎯ cared, ⎯ guard, ⎯ great, ⎯ called, ⎯ cold or equalled, ⎯ gold, ⎯ cannot, ⌄ gentleman, ⌄ gentlemen, ⎯ happened, ⎯ particular, ⎯ opportunity, ⎯ child, ⎯ not.

LESSON 27. ⎯ build-ing or able to, ⎯ told or till it, ⎯ tried, ⎯ toward or trade, ⌄ did not, ⌄ had not or do not, ⎯ chaired, ⎯ cheered, ⎯ if it, ⎯ that, (without, ⎯ third, ⎯ sent, ⎯ somewhat, ⎯ short, ⎯ met, ⎯ meeting.

LESSON 28. ⎯ spirit, ⎯ may not, ⎯ hand, ⎯ under, ⎯ yard, ⎯ word, ⎯ wonderful-ly.

LESSON 29. ⎯ school, ⎯ schooled, ⎯ commercial, ⎯ financial, ⎯ especial-ly, ⎯ influential, ⎯ uninfluential, ⎯ substantial-ly, ⎯ unsubstantial-ly, ⎯ controversy-sial, ⎯ circumstance, ⎯ circumstantial, ⎯ immediate, ⎯ immediately, ⎯ prejudice-cial.

LESSON 30. ⎯ passenger, ⎯ danger, ⎯ dangerous, ⎯ stranger, ⎯ messenger, ⎯ manuscript, ⎯ transcribe, ⎯ transcript, ⎯ transcription, ⎯ transfer, ⎯ transgress, ⎯ transgression, ⎯ transmission, ⎯ understand, ⎯ understood, ⎯ whenever, ⎯ whatever.

GRAMMALOGS AND CONTRACTIONS.

LESSON 31. better than, rather than, rather *or* writer, perform-ed, performer, performs-ance, reform-ed, reformer, reformation, inform-ed, informer, information, thankful, thanksgiving.

LESSON 33. proficient-cy-ly, deficient-cy-ly, efficient-cy-ly, inefficient-cy-ly, sufficient-cy-ly, insufficient-cy-ly, observation, preservation, electric, electrical, electricity, inconsiderate, selfish-ness, unselfish-ness.

LESSON 34. never, nevertheless, notwithstanding, enlarge, enlarged, probable-ly-ility, practice *or* practise-d, practicable, imperfect-ion, satisfaction, satisfactory, unsatisfactory.

LESSON 35. mistake, mistaken, domestic, character, characteristic, description, justification, generalization, organize-d, organization, extinguish-ed, distinguish-ed, relinquish-ed, covenant, govern-ed, government, magnetic-ism,

LESSON 36. captain, capable, incapable, appointment, disappointment, attainment *or* atonement, entertainment, contentment, indignant-ation, resignation, antagonist-ic-ism, inscribe-d, inscription, instructive, instruction.

LESSON 37. discharge-d, displeasure, dissimilar, expenditure, expensive, extraordinary, extravagant-ce, manufacture-d, manufacturer, intelligent, intelligence, intelligible, advertise-d-ment.

LESSON 38. individual, investment, interest, interested, uninteresting, disinterested-ness, applicable-ility, astonish-ed-ment, certificate, contingency.

LESSON 39. demonstrate, remonstrate, ministry, familiar-ity, preliminary, singular, indispensable-ly.

LESSON 40. indescribable, indiscriminate, sensible-ility, peculiar-ity, perpendicular, proportion-ed, proportionate-ly, establish-ed-ment.

FIFTY PRINCIPAL CITIES ARRANGED ACCORDING TO POPULATION

New York (N. Y.)
Chicago (Ill.).....
Philadelphia (Pa.).
St. Louis (Mo.)...
Boston (Mass.)...
Baltimore (Md.)..
Cleveland (Ohio)..
Buffalo (N. Y.)....
San Francisco (Cal.)
Cincinnati (Ohio)..
Pittsburg (Pa.)....
New Orleans (La.)
Detroit (Mich.)...
Milwaukee (Wis.).
Washington (D. C.)
Newark (N. J.)....
Jersey City (N. J.)
Louisville (Ky.)...
Minneapolis (Minn.)
Providence (R. I.).
Indianapolis (Ind.)
Kansas City (Mo.)
St. Paul (Minn.)...
Rochester (N. Y.).
Denver (Colo.)....
Toledo (Ohio).....
Allegheny (Pa.)...
Columbus (Ohio)..
Worcester (Mass.).
Syracuse (N. Y.).
New Haven (Conn.
Paterson (N. J.)...
Fall River (Mass.).
St. Joseph (Mo.)..
Omaha (Neb.)....
Los Angeles (Cal.)
Memphis (Tenn.)..
Scranton (Pa.)....
Lowell (Mass.)....
Albany (N. Y.)....
Cambridge (Mass.)
Portland (Ore.)...
Atlanta (Ga.).....
Grand Rapids (Mich.).
Dayton (Ohio)....
Richmond (Va.)...
Nashville (Tenn.).
Seattle (Wash.)....
Hartford (Conn.)..
Reading (Pa.).....

CONTRACTIONS FOR NAMES OF STATES AND TERRITORIES

Officially adopted by the United States Post Office Department.

Ala.		Mont.	
Alaska		Nebr.	
Ariz.		Nev.	
Ark.		N. H.	
Cal.		N. J.	
C. Z.		N. Mex.	
Colo.		N. Y.	
Conn.		N. C.	
Del.		N. Dak.	
D. C.		Ohio	
Fla.		Okla.	
Ga.		Oregon	
Idaho		Pa.	
Ill.		R. I.	
Ind.		S. C.	
Iowa		S. Dak.	
Kans.		Tenn.	
Ky.		Tex.	
La.		Utah	
Maine		Vt.	
Md.		Va.	
Mass.		Wash.	
Mich.		W. Va.	
Minn.		Wis.	
Miss.		Wyo.	
Mo.			

GRAMMALOGS.

ARRANGED ALPHABETICALLY.

a *or* an		called		equal-ly	
able		can		equalled	
above		cannot		ever-y	
accord-ing		care		evil	
advantage		cared		eye	
ago		cart		first	
ah !		chair		for	
all		chaired		from	
and		cheer		general-ly	
any		cheered		generaliza- tion	
apply		child			
approve		children		generation	
are		Christian-ity		gentleman	
as		circumstance		gentlemen	
at		circumstan- [ces		give-n	
aught		cold		go	
awe		come		gold	
ay (yes)		constitution al-ly		great	
aye				greatest	
balance		could		guard	
balanced		dear		had	
balances		deliver-ed-y		half	
be		deliverance		hand	
because		difference-t		happen	
been		difficult		happened	
behalf		do		happy	
belief-ve-d		doctor, Dr.		has	
beyond		dollar, dollars		have	
build-ing		done		he	
but		down		heaven	
buy bye		during		high	
by		each		him	
call		eh ?		himself	

his		me		particular	
holy		meeting		people	
hour		member		phonography	
house		mere		pleasure	
how		met		principal-ly	
however		more		principle	
I		most		put	
if [ant		Mr.		quite	
importance-		much		rather	
impossible		must		religion	
improve-d-ment		my		religious	
		myself		remark-ed	
improves-ments		near		remember-ed	
		next		satisfaction	
in		no		Saviour	
influence		nor		saw	
influenced		northern		school	
information		not		schooled	
initial-ly-ed		number-ed		Scripture	
inscribe-d		O! oh!		sea	
inscription		of		see	
instruction		often		selfish-ness	
instructive		on		sent	
is		one		several	
it		opinion		shall, shalt	
itself		opportunity		short	
journal		or		should	
justification		other		significance	
know		ought		significant	
language		our		signification	
large		ourselves		signify-ied	
largely		out		so	
larger		over		somewhat	
liberty		owe		southern	
Lord		owing		speak	
may		own		special-ly	

GRAMMALOGS.

spirit		though		what	
strength		threw		when	
subject-ed		through		whether	
subjection		thus		which	
subjective		thyself		while	
suggest-ed		till		whither	
suggestion		to		who	
suggestive		to be		whose	
sure		told		why	
surprise		too		will	
surprised		towards		wish	
tell		trade		with	
thank-ed		tried		within	
that		true		without	
the		truth		wonderful-ly	
their		try		word	
them		two		would	
themselves		under		writer	
there		up		yard	
therefore		upon		ye	
these		us		year	
they		usual-ly		yes	
thing		valuation		you	
think		very		young	
third		was		your	
this		way		youth	
those		we		youths	

LIST OF CONTRACTIONS.
ARRANGED ALPHABETICALLY.

The following list contains also the Contractions which appear in "Pitman's Shorthand Instructor."

abandonment		baptize-d-st-ism	
abstraction		benevolent-ce	
abstractive		benignant-ity	
acknowledge		bondservant	
acknowledged		bondsman	
acknowledgment		cabinet	
administrate		Calvinism	
administration		capable	
administrative		captain	
administrator		catholic	
administratrix		certificate	
advertise-d-ment		character	
agriculture-al		characteristic	
altogether		circumstantial	
amalgamate		commercial	
amalgamation		contentment	
antagonist-ic-		contingency	
anything [ism		controversy-ial	
applicable-ility		covenant [tion	
appointment		cross-examina-	
arbitrament		cross-examine-d	
arbitrary		danger	
arbitrate		dangerous	
arbitration		defective	
arbitrator		deficient-cy	
archbishop		degeneration	
architect-ure-al		delinquency	
aristocracy-atic		delinquent	
assignment		democracy-atic	
astonish-ed-ment		demonstrate	
atonement		demonstration	
attainment		denomination-al	
auspicious		denominational- ism	
bankruptcy			

depreciate-d
depreciatory
description
destruction
destructive
destructively
dethronement
difficulty
dignify-ied-ty
dilapidate-d-ion
disappointment
discharge-d
disinterested-ness
displeasure
disproportion-ed
disproportionate
disrespect
disrespectful
dissimilar
distinguish-ed
doctrine
ecclesiastic-al
efficient-cy
electric
electrical
electricity
emergency
England
English
Englishman
enlarge
enlarged
enlargement
enlarger
enlightenment
entertainment
enthusiastic-ism
Episcopal-ian-ism
especial
esquire
establish-ed-ment
evangelical
everything
exchange-d
executive
executor
executrix
expect-ed
expediency
expenditure
expensive
extemporaneous
extinguish-ed
extraordinary
extravagant-ance
falsification
familiar-ity
familiarization
familiarize
February
financial
govern-ed
government
henceforth
henceforward.
howsoever
identical
immediate
imperfect-ion

- imperturbable
- impracticable
- impregnable
- improbable-ility
- incandescence
- incandescent
- incapable
- inconsiderate
- inconvenience-t
- incorporated
- indefatigable
- independent-ce
- indescribable
- indignant-ion
- indiscriminate
- indispensable
- individual
- inefficient-cy
- influential
- inform-ed
- informer
- insignificance
- insignificant
- inspect-ed-ion
- insubordinate-ion
- insufficient-cy
- insurance
- intelligence
- intelligent
- intelligible
- interest
- interested
- introduction
- investigation
- investment
- ironmonger
- irrecoverable
- irregular
- irremovable
- irrespective
- irrespectively
- irresponsible-[ility
- January
- journalism
- journalistic
- jurisdiction
- jurisprudence
- knowledge
- legislative
- legislature
- magnetic-ism
- manufacture-d
- manufacturer
- manuscript
- marconigram
- mathematic-al-s
- mathematician
- maximum
- mechanical
- melancholy
- messenger
- Methodism
- metropolitan
- minimum
- ministration
- ministry
- minstrel
- misdemeanour
- misfortune
- misrepresent-ed
- monstrosity

CONTRACTED WORDS.

monstrous		phonographic	
mortgage-d		platform	
neglect-ed		plenipotentiary	
negligence		practicable	
never		practice	
nevertheless		practise-d	
nonconformist		prejudice-d-ial	
nonconformity		preliminary	
nothing		prerogative	
notwithstanding		Presbyterian-ism	
November		preservation	
object-ed		probable-ility	
objection		production	
objectionable		productive	
objective		proficient-cy	
obscurity		project-ed	
observation		proportion-ed	
obstruction		proportionate	
obstructive		prospect	
oneself		prospective	
organization		prospectus	
organize-d		public	
organizer		publication	
orthodox-y		publish-ed	
parliamentarian		publisher	
parliamentary		questionable	
passenger		ratepayers	
peculiar-ity		recognizance	
perform-ed		recoverable	
performer		reform-ed	
performs-ance		reformation	
perpendicular		reformer	
perspective		regular	
philanthropist		relinquish-ed	
philanthropy-ic		remarkable	
phonographer		remonstrance	

remonstrant	
remonstrate	
removable	
represent-ed	
representation	
representative	
reproduction	
reproductive	
republic	
republican	
repugnance-ant	
resignation	
respect-ed	
respectful	
respective	
respectively	
responsible-ility	
resurrection	
retrospect	
retrospection	
retrospective	
retrospectively	
reverend	
satisfactory	
sensible-ility	
singular	
something	
stranger	
stringency	
subscribe-d	
subscription	
substantial	
sufficient-cy	
suspect-ed	
sympathetic	
tabernacle	
telegram	
telegraphic	
thankful	
thanksgiving	
thenceforward	
together [tion	
transubstantia-	
tribunal	
unanimity	
unanimous	
unconstitutional	
unexpected-ly	
uniform-ity	
uninfluential	
uninteresting	
universal	
universality	
Universalism	
universe	
university	
unprincipled	
unquestionable	
unsatisfactory	
unselfish-ness	
unsubstantial	
unsuspected	
unsympathetic	
vegetarian	
vegetarianism	
whatever	
whenever	
whensoever	
whereinsoever	
wheresoever	
whithersoever	
yesterday	

THE PHONOGRAPHIC ALPHABET.
CONSONANTS.

Names.				Names.			
pee	P	\	as in rope	ef	F	⌒	as in safe
bee	B	\	,, robe	vee	V	⌒	,, save
tee	T	|	,, fate	ith	TH	(	,, wreath
dee	D	|	,, fade	thee	TH	(	,, wreathe
chay	CH	/	,, choke	es	S	)°	,, hiss
jay	J	/	,, joke	zee	Z	)	,, his
kay	K	—	,, leek	ish	SH	)	,, vicious
gay	G	—	,, league	zhee	ZH	)	,, vision
em	M	⌒	,, seem	el	L	((up stroke)	as in pall
en	N	⌣	,, seen	ar	R	\ (down stroke)	,, air
ing	NG	⌣	,, sing	ray	R	/ (up stroke)	,, raise
way	W	✓	,, way	hay	{ H ? (down stroke) / H ◡ (up stroke) }		,, high
yay	Y	✓	,, yea				

VOWELS.

	Long.		sign (heavy)		Short.		sign (light)
1 ah	1 aw	1	• —	1 ă	1 ŏ	1	• —
2 ā	2 ō	2	• —	2 ě	2 ŭ	2	• —
3 ē	3 ōō	3	• —	3 ĭ	3 ŏŏ	3	• —

as in \ bah, \ bay, \ bee, as in ⌢ lass, ⌢ less, ⌢ lisp,
⌒ law, ⌒ low, ⌒ loo. ⌣ boss, ⌣ bus, ⌣ puss.

DIPHTHONGS.

Sign v ∧ ⌐ ⌒   as in \ pie, \ bough,
Sound ī ow oi ū.   ⌐ toy, ⌣ due,

TABLE OF SINGLE AND DOUBLE CONSONANTS.

		L hook.	R hook.	N hook.	F and V hook.	Half Length
P	\	pl	pr	pn	pf	pt
B	\	bl	br	bn	bf	bd
T	|	tl	tr	tn	tf	tt
D	|	dl	dr	dn	df	dd
CH	/	chl	chr	chn	chf	cht
J	/	jl	jr	jn	jf	jd
K	—	kl	kr	kn	kf	kt
G	—	gl	gr	gn	gf	gd
F	\	fl	fr	fn	....	ft
V	\	vl	vr	vn	....	vd
TH	(	thl	thr	thn	....	tht
TH	(	thl	thr	thn	....	thd
S, Z	))	....	....	sn) zn)	....	st) zd)
SH	)	shl up,down	shr down,up	shn down,up	....	sht
ZH	)	....	zhr	zhn	....	zhd
M	⌒	ml	mr	mn	....	mt / md
N	⌣	nl	nr	nn	....	nt / nd
NG	⌣	....	ng'r	ngn	....	
L	(	....	....	ln up,down	....	lt / ld down
R	/ up	....	....	rn up	rf	rt
R	\	....	....	rn	....	rt / rd
W		....	....	wn	wf	wt
Y		....	....	yn	yf	yt
H	9	....	....	hn	hf	ht

KW	GW	WL	WHL	LR	RR	MP or MB	WH
		up	up	down	down		

LIST OF PHRASEOGRAMS.

Not including the Phrases indicated in the ordinary type given in preceding pages.

- additional cost
- additional expense
- and if you should be
- and the contrary
- as we can
- as we have
- as we think
- as soon as
- as soon as convenient
- as well as
- at any rate
- at all events
- at all times
- at once
- at some time
- at the same time
- at your early convenience
- Bank of New York
- before him
- before there is
- best class
- best of my ability
- best of our ability
- best of their ability
- best of your ability
- Dear Sir
- deliver immediately
- Dramatic Society
- early consideration
- early reply
- enclose-d herewith
- facts of the case
- first class
- for some time
- for the first time
- for the sake of
- for their sake
- from first to last
- from time to time
- further consideration
- further considered
- general manager
- having regard to
- Hazell & Co.
- he is the

how can they
I am
I am content
I am directed to state
I am in receipt of your favor
I am in receipt of your esteemed favor
I am instructed to state
I am not
I am requested to state
I am sorry
I am surprised
I am very sorry
I ask attention
I can
I can assure you
I do not *or* I had not
I do not understand
I did not
I have
I have arranged
I have concluded
I have had
I have received
I have the
I have to inform you
I hope you will

I hope you will not
I may
I may be
I know there is
I regard
I regret
I say
I see
I shall arrange
I shall be compelled
I shall be pleased
I thank you
I think
I think the
I think you should be
I will
I will be
if it
if it is
if you should be
in consequence
in regard to
in relation to
in reply
In reply to your esteemed favor

in reply to your favor
in the first place
in this city
in which it is
it is said
it is the
it must be
it would be
Jones Publishing Co.
Journal of Commerce
just possible
just received
Knox & Co.
last month
last time
last week
less and less
local authority
medical authorities
Monday morning
more and more
more or less
my attention has been called
National Bank

next time
next week
on the contrary
party question
Pennsylvania R.R.
Pitman's Journal
please forward
please inform us
please let me know
please let us know
please make arrangements
please note
please quote us
political party
referring to your favor
referring to yours
respectfully yours
satisfactory conclusion
shall be taken into consideration
shipping department
side by side
South Carolina R.R.
take-n into consideration
this is

this week
to go
to him
to the contrary
Tuesday afternoon
under the circumstances
United States
unsatisfactory conclusion
very truly yours
wagon department
we are in a position
we are sorry
Wednesday evening
what can be
what do you
when the
when they
what may be
why do you
why have you
with each
with much
with reference to
with regard to

with relation to
with respect to
with the
with which
yesterday afternoon
you are not
you can
you may
you may as well
you may be
you may not
you must receive
you should be
you were not
you will
you will be
you will comply
you will not
your esteemed favor
your favor
your reply
yours respectfully
yours truly

BUSINESS CORRESPONDENCE.
(1.)

Messrs. Kingsley & Sons,
    Toledo, Ohio.

Dear-Sirs:

We-are-much-obliged · *for-your*-letter *of-the* 14th, *with*--reference-*to-the* new machine *which-we-have*-just placed *on-the* market. *We-are*-pleased *to know that-you-are so* thoroughly satisfied *with-it, and-we should*-feel still-further obliged *if-you would* kindly permit *us to*-reproduce *your*--letter *in-the* new *advertising* booklet *we-are*-preparing *to* issue *in-the*-early autumn. *We-have* already received permission *to* incorporate letters *from*-many *of-our* clients, *and-we* confidently anticipate *your* kind sanction *to* add *yours.*

Regarding *your* note *as-to-the* despatch *of-your* last-order, *we have* made inquiries *and*-find *that-the special* parts *you*--mention were undoubtedly packed *in-the* largest *of-the* three cases *sent to-you on-the* 11th *inst.* *We-have-no*-doubt *that* further inquiry *at-your* end *will* confirm *this*-statement.

With-regard-*to your* order *No.* 546, *we*-hope *to-be in a* position *to* despatch *the* whole *of-the* pulleys *on or* before-*the* 28th *inst.*

                                   Yours-truly,

[183

(2.)

Messrs. Drake & Swan,
    Cumberland, Ind.

Gentlemen:

We-have-your-favor *of-the* 20th *instant, together with* -check *for* $78.50, *for-which* please accept *our* best-thanks. Formal receipt is-enclosed-herewith along-*with* advice--note *of-the* goods *which-have* gone forward *to*-day, *and*-.*which-we*-trust *you-will*-find *satisfactory in-every-way.*

Our representative visits *your* district twice *a year, and--will in-*future *call-upon you,* advising *you* some-time *in--*advance. Any orders *with-which-you-may* favor *us through-him will-be* executed *on* journey terms, namely, six-months'-account less 5% discount.

Yours-respectfully,

[100

(3.)

Mr. Paul Dootson,
    St. Louis, Mo.

*Dear-*Sir:

With further-reference *to-our* conversation *with-you on-the* 6th *inst., we-have* reconsidered *the* question *of-your* contract, *and-we very-much* regret *that-we-do-not-see our--way to-*renew *it on-the* conditions *at-*present *in-*force. *Our* calculations show *that-we-have* lost considerably *by--the* agreement, *so-that-we-are-*obliged *to-*terminate-*the* same. *You-will, therefore,* please-take formal notice *that under-the-*terms named *in* Clause 5 *of-the* contract *we--shall* discontinue *the* supply *of* coal *to-you, at-the-*prices charged *under-the* contract *in-*question, *on* March 25 *next, on which* date *the* said contract *will* expire.

*We-shall-be very-*pleased *to-*discuss-*the* question *of a* new contract *with you on* revised terms *and* conditions, *and-if--you-will* make-(an)-*appointment,* our *Mr.* Barnet *will-be--*glad *to-call-upon you.*

Respectfully-yours,

[158

(4.)

The Ellison Bicycle Store,
    Elmira, *N. Y.*

*Dear-*Sirs:

*We-have-your-*favor of July 31, enclosing advices *of* accessories despatched *in* compliance *with our* instructions.

and-we-are-much-obliged *for-your* prompt-attention. *With--reference-to your* remarks about-*the number of* inquiries *you*-receive direct *from this* district, *the* matter *is* easily explained. *There-is a belief largely* prevalent *that by* dealing *with* headquarters direct buyers save ten *or* fifteen per--cent. *We*-propose *shortly to* issue *a* circular-letter *to--remove this* wrong idea, *and-we*-trust *you-will* afterwards cease *to-be* troubled *with-these* inquiries.

We-have-had two-(or)-three complaints regarding-*the* finish *of-the* last consignment *of* "Climbers." Perhaps *you-will* look into-(the)-matter, *and* see *if-there-is-any* ground *for-the* complaints?

We-enclose-herewith *a* further batch *of*-orders *for-the* No. 4 "Star Cycles," *and-we-shall-be*-glad *if-you-will--arrange to-deliver these* strictly *on* time, *as they-are* urgently wanted.

Respectfully-yours,

[170

(5.)

Mr. William Harrison,
    Chicago, Ill.

Dear-Sir:

We-have-your-favor *of-the* 20th *instant*, enclosing-check value $370.15, *in* settlement-(of)-account, *and for--which-we-thank-you*. *We-are*-sorry *that-you do-not* consider lot 543 good value, *but-we*-feel *sure we-could-not--have* got *it at-the*-price *if-it-had-not-been that-the*-majority *of-the* buyers were *overstocked.* Similar lots *went* off easily *at higher*-rates. *We*-feel *sure, however, that on-the* whole *we-have* executed *your* commission *to-your satisfaction, and-that-you-will* entrust *us with* similar commissions *in the* future.

Respectfully-yours,

[106

(6.)

Mr. Reuben Shaw,
    Indianapolis, Ind.

*Dear-*Sir:

We-have-carefully-considered the question raised *by--our* Mr. Johnson, namely, *that-we should* grant *you a* discount *of* 10% *on our* account, *and-we-*regret *to* say *that-we-do-not at-*present *see our-way to-*offer *you more--than-the* 5% *you* now receive. *We-may, however,* add *that should our* account *with you* reach-*the* sum *of* $2,500 *a year we-shall-be-*pleased *to* increase-*the* discount allowed *you to* 7½%; *while, if-the-*account *should* reach $5,000 *a year, we should* then *be-able-to* raise *the* discount *to* 10%. W*e-would* remind *you that yours is a* six-months'-account, *and-we-think-you-will-*agree *that-this-is* long-credit.

Respectfully-yours,

[128

(7.)

Mr. Peter Bennett,
    Cleveland, Ohio.

*Dear-*Sir:

Referring *to-our* conversation here *on-the* 17th *inst., we should-be-*glad *if-you would* kindly sign-*the* enclosed formal agreement embodying-*the* terms *already* verbally agreed *to. As you-are* aware, *we* require *you to-*take *up-the* duties *of-the* appointment *on-the* 1st of July, *without* fail, *and-we-*hope *to-*hear *that-you-will-be* prepared *to-do-so.* Please supply *us immediately with a* list *of-your* requirements *in-the-way-*of stationery, etc., *so-that-we-may* get *these in-*hand *and-have everything* ready *for-the* 1st of July.

Yours-truly,

[104

(8.)

Mr. Edward Lowther,
    Toledo, Ohio.

Dear-Sir:

Your-letter *of*-March 30 came duly *to hand, and--we-thank-you* sincerely *for-your suggestion, which shall* receive *our most careful* consideration. *You-may* depend *upon-it that-we-shall-not* forget *you should there-be anything in-your* line *in-the* future. *It-is a* curious fact *that--we* frequently receive *suggestions for-the*-same *thing from* two or more correspondents *at-the*-same-time. *It-is-so-in-this*-case. *A* fortnight *ago a* correspondent offered *us a* scheme practically *the* same *as your-own, and he-is to*-submit full details *in-the*-course *of a* few-days. *Whether we-shall-do anything with-it or not, we-cannot at*-present say. *We-will* write-*you* again *in a* week *or so.*

            Yours-truly,

                        [136

(9.)

Mr. S. Wilson,
    Omaha, Nebr.

Dear-Sir:

We-thank-you for-your-favor *of-the* 10th *instant. It--appears to us, however, that-it-would-be much-more to--your advantage to* obtain *your* supplies *nearer* home, *as your* orders *would-not, in-all-probability, be large* enough *to* warrant *the* expense *of* expressage. *We*-enclose-here-with *a list of*-dealers *who* buy *in* bulk *from us, who* stock practically *all-our* leading lines, and *who-would very*-likely offer-*you* terms *that-would* suit *you.*

            Respectfully-yours,

                        [88

(10.)

Messrs. Hill & Blears,
    Liverpool, England.

Gentlemen:

*We-thank-you for-your-*letter *of-the* 12th *inst., and for-the* promptness *with-which-you* acceded *to-our* request *to* act *as our representatives on-the* Liverpool market. *We-*agree *to-the-*terms named *in-your-*letter, *and-have* already, *as* advised *by* cable, made *you a* consignment *of* 550 bales. *The* cost-price, *as* shown *on* enclosed *Pro--forma* Invoice amounts *to* $8.70, *and-we-*trust *that your* market *will improve at-*least *a* few points before-*the* consignment arrives, *to-*day's quotations *being very* discouraging. *We-have-*drawn *on-the* Bank-*of-*Liverpool, *as* authorized *by-you, for* 80% *of* Invoice, viz., £3,950. Bill *of* Lading *and Certificate of Insurance are* attached *to-*draft. *We-shall-be-*glad *if-you-will* remit further proceeds *by* cable transfer. Copies *of* cablegrams enclosed.

Yours-truly,

[143

(11.)

Mr. R. Goodman,
    Hillsboro, N. H.

*Dear-*Sir:

We-thank-you for-yours of-the 25th *inst., with* order *No.* 786, *which-has-been* mailed *to-*day. *The information you-give with-*regard-to E. H. *is more* favorable than *the* report furnished *us by* Black's Agency. Please look into--*the* case *very carefully and* make some further inquiries *as to-his* reliability, *and* advise *us if-you think it-would--be* safe *to-*grant *the* credit desired. *We-shall-not* forward *the* goods until *we-have-your* further-letter.

Yours-truly,

[91

(12.)

Mr. W. Davis,
    Chicago, Ill.

Dear-Sir:

Referring-*to-your*-favor *of-the* 10th *inst.*, *we*-regret *that-the* alternative *you* offer *would-not* suit *our* purpose *at-all, while-the* price *you* quote *for a special* lot *is much beyond what we-have* previously paid. Such *a* figure *would* compel *us to* name *a* price *for our* work *which-would-give us no* hope *of* obtaining *any of-the large* contracts *for-which-we* desire *to* compete. *If-you-cannot* revise *your*-terms *we-must* look elsewhere *for our* requirements.

                       Yours-respectfully,

[93

(13.)

Messrs. Turner & Smith,
    Rome, *N. Y.*

Gentlemen:

Yours of-the 12th *inst. to hand this* morning. In--face *of-the* increased rates now ruling *in-almost every* branch *of-the trade, we*-assure-*you it-is-quite-impossible to*-quote former prices *to-our* customers, *and-in* raising *our* quotations *we-have-only* followed-*the* example *of-every other-manufacturer. We-are* willing, *however, to*-make *a* sacrifice *so-as-to* enable-*you to* compete favorably *for-the* contracts referred *to in-your*-letter. *We-shall, therefore,* let *you have-the special* line *as* per sample enclosed *with our-letter of-the* 10th *inst., at-the* reduced rate *of* 25 cents per lb., *in-not*-less-than five-ton lots. Please wire *us on* receipt *of-this*-letter *if-you*-agree, *as* prices *are* likely *to-go* up further *in a* day *or-two.*

                       Yours-truly,

[143

(14.)

Messrs. King & Pearce,
    Albany, N. Y.

Dear Sirs:

We should-feel extremely-obliged *for-your opinion* regarding-*the general* standing, reliability, *and* solvency *of-the* person named *on-the* accompanying slip. *This--gentleman has-been a* customer *of-ours for-years, and*--until recently *has always met his* engagements punctually. Lately, *however, we*-find *it* exceedingly *difficult to* obtain *a* settlement *of-our* account *with him*. *We-shall, of*-course, regard *your information as* absolutely confidential, *and-we-shall-be*-glad *to*-return-*the* service, *should* occasion arise. *Thank*ing *you in*-advance,

Yours-respectfully,

[95

(15.)

Messrs. Schuster & Co.,
    New-York, N. Y.

Gentlemen:

As I-have frequently *to*-make *large* purchases *of* dye--stuffs *in* Germany, *and* am consequently *under-the* necessity *of* remitting considerable sums *to-that* country, *I should* like *to*-find *a more* advantageous method *of* doing-*so* than-*the* purchase *of*-drafts *from-my* local banker, *who* charges *what I*-consider *an* unduly *high* commission *for-the* service. *Will-you* please-*inform-me if-you would-be* disposed *to* effect such remittances *at-the* prevailing market rates? *I-will*-forward *my* check *on-my* local bank *when* instructing *you to*-remit, *and-I*-am-confident *that any*-inquiry *you-may*-make here *will* prove *to-you the* perfect safety *of*-such transactions *with me*. Trusting *to*-receive *an* early-reply,

Yours-respectfully,

[131

(16.)

The General Manager,
　　Sun-Blind-Co.,-Ltd.,
　　　　Brooklyn, *N. Y.*

Dear-Sir:

We-are-obliged *for-your* check *in-part* payment *of-*
-our account *up to* June 31 last, *and-we* return-*the* statement herewith, duly receipted. *We* also beg-*to*-enclose-
-herewith copies *of-the* invoices *which-you have* struck *out,*
and-we-shall feel obliged *if-you-will* kindly forward remittance *for-the balance at-your*-earliest-convenience, *so-that-*
-we-may clear *our* books. *We*-regret *that-we-cannot* allow *the* contra deductions *you have* made. *These* evidently concern *our* City Branch, *and-as their*-accounts *are quite* distinct *from ours your* invoice *should-be-sent to-them* direct.

　　　　　　　Yours-truly,

[114

ON OBSERVATION.

(From "The Business Life," by W. Gamble.)

One of-the most indispensable faculties *in*-Business *is-that of Observation. It-is indispensable in every* occupation. *Without-it, a* man *goes through* life contending against *great* odds. *He-is always* blundering *into* difficulties, *always up to-the* chin *in a sea of*-troubles, *always* losing valuable *hours and* days *of-his*-life, *and* wasting money *in* pursuits *which*-might *be* avoided *by-the* exercise *of-this* inestimable faculty.

There-are so-many men *who go through* life *with* eyes *and* ears open, *yet, so to speak,* neither *seeing nor* hearing *anything. They* knock *their* heads against *a* pillar *or a* brick-wall *for-want-of* necessary *observation to* teach *them* where *to-expect to*-find *a* pillar *or a* brick-wall; *and* even *with-the* unpleasant experience *which* such contact entails *they*-take such little *advantage of Observation that-*
-they blunder *into-the*-same *obstruction the next*-day.

An old *sea captain who-was* asked *if-he* knew where-*the* rocks were *in a* certain harbor, showed *his* keen sense *of Observation when-he* replied, "*No*, sir, *but I know* where *they* ain't."

But whilst *Observation* teaches *us what to* avoid; *it also* prompts *us to-the* achievement *of-great things.* Genius, Talent, Inventiveness, *Knowledge,* Experience, *are* synonymous *with Observation.*

Consider-*the* lives *of-the great-*men *of-this or any other* age, *and-it-will* invariably *be-*found *that-their greatness* arose *from-their* possession *of-the* faculty *of Observation-which* led *them to* conceive some *great* invention *or* make some grand discovery, *owing to-*some simple *circumstance which had* impressed *itself on-their* minds, whilst *other* men *would-have* left *it* unnoticed. Sir Isaac Newton *saw an* apple fall *to-the* ground, *as* multitudes *have-*seen apples fall; *but-the* fact impressed *itself on-his-*mind, *and* led *him to* evolve *the* law *of-*gravitation *with-its* ceaseless *influence over* (the) world of-matter. Watt made *his first* successful steam-engine *through* watching *the* steam issue *from a* kettle; *and-one of-the greatest improvements in-the-*early steam-engine *was* discovered *by a* lazy, *but* observant boy, *who-was* set *to* pull *a* string *to* actuate *a* lever, *and-*found-*the* work *was* just *as-well* accomplished *by* tying *the* string *to* another lever, *so-that he-was* left free *to-go* off *and-*play marbles. *These and* similar examples *which-*might *be* indefinitely multiplied, *are* illustrations *of-that Observation which usually distinguishes* successful *people.*

Observation is usually and most appropriately associated *with seeing. We speak of a* clever-man *as one* "*with all--his* eyes about-*him*" *or* "*who goes* about-*the-*world *with--his* eyes open," *and-we-have-*heard *it remarked of a* man *that* "*he* keeps *his* eyes peeled." *But it-wants something--more-than mere* seeing *to-be* observant; *the* vision *must-be* mental *as-well-as* physical. *The* divine proverb says,

"*The* wise man's eyes *are in-his* head," *and-we-know what that* means. *There-are-*many men *who* act *as-though-their* eyes were *in-their-*feet, *or their* elbows; *or any*where, *in* fact, *but* where-*they ought-to-be. A* Russian proverb says, "*He goes through-the* forest *and sees no* firewood." *The* mind *must-see as-well-as-the eye; and-the* wise-man employs *not his* vision alone, *but all-his* powers, *so-as-to--make-the* most *of-his-*life. *A* fool *can* behold *an object; but-that-is all. The* act *does-not* make *him* wiser *or* better. *He-is a* fool; *and* continues foolish amongst scenes *that ought to-*lift *him to a* nobler manhood.

It may-be urged *that-the* faculty *of Observation is a* natural gift, *and so no-*doubt *it-is; but if-it-is-not* born *in a* man, *or if-it-be* small *and* weak *in-him, it can be* cultivated *as other* weak powers *are* cultivated. *It-has--been* well said *that-the* habit *of* sharp discriminating *Observation may-be established by* perseverance, *as other* good habits *become* permanent. Thousands *of-*men *go through-the-*world *without* learning, *or* even trying *to--*learn, *how* some-men succeed, *and why others* fail. *They* ascribe Success *to* "Luck" *and* Failure *to* unavoidable "*misfortune.*" *Others, a* little wiser, set *it down to-*lack *of* education; *but-this* alone *is-not-the-*cause, *for there-are--many-instances of-*men *of-the* most meagre education *who-have* risen *to high* positions *and-*even world-wide fame. Lord Bacon said: "Studies teach *not their-own* use; *but-there-is a* wisdom *without-them, and above them* won *by observation.*"

*In-the-*workshops *of to-*day *we-*want *young-*men *who-will* ask *themselves why the* wheels *go* round, *why one* wheel *goes* faster *or* slower than-another, *why one way of-doing a thing is better-than* another, *and why the* act *of-doing one thing* brings about *a* certain result; *young-*men, *in-*fact, *who-can always see that-there-are always more ways of-*doing *a thing, and can* decide *which-way is* best; also reflecting *that if* another-*way could-be* discovered *it-*might *be* better still.

We often hear *it* discussed *what* technical *schools ought to* teach. *The* answer *is* simple. Let *them* teach Resourcefulness *and Observation and how to* attain *these* accomplishments.

When young-men step *out* into-*the*-world *to* shift *for--themselves, the* value *of Observation* soon makes *itself* felt; *and*-only *those* really succeed *who know how to* observe *the* tendencies *of* acts; *who-can* read *and* value *character* properly; *who* discern *the* signs *of-the* times; *who-are equal to-emergencies; who-can* husband resources; *and who know how to-do-the* right *thing at-the* right time *and--in-the* right *place. These* qualities only *come of* cultivating *the* faculty *of Observation.* Smart men *are* only men *of* keen *Observation, who-can* take *in a* situation *at a* glance, *and* act quickly *on-the* impulse *of-the* moment.

ON OPPORTUNITY.

(From "The Business Life," by W. Gamble.)

"Opportunity is a great thing," so-the old saying *goes. True, but-the* ability *to-*grasp *opportunities is of-great*er *importance. Opportunities come to-most of us—we may--*say, indeed, *to all of us—but*-some *people never see an opportunity, while others see but* ignore *it.* Some *think they can put it* aside *to-*take *advantage of-it at a more* favorable time, like-*the* dog *who* hides *his* bone *and,* also like-*the* dog, either forgetting *it or* finding *that* another *has* run off *with-it.*

*To-*many *people an opportunity comes as* such *a* solid *and* tangible *thing that-they* knock *their* heads against *it, or* fall *over-it, yet they* only thrust *or* kick *it* aside *with* perhaps *a* curse *at it. Others* profess *to-be always* looking *for an opportunity,* yet lamenting-*the* fact *that-they never* find *it, and it never comes to-them.* Some *are* foolish enough *to-believe that-they can buy opportunities, and* stand *in-the*-market-place jingling *their*-money *in-their--pockets* until *a* sharp-witted rogue *sees his opportunity and*-takes-*it*.

There-is yet another-class *who-have* aptitude enough *to see an opportunity, but who* only take hold *of-it and* carry *it to a half-way house, when-they* begin *to*-find *it-is too* heavy *for-them*. They feel thirsty *and*-want *a* drink *and a* rest; *they* leave *their opportunity* outside, *so to-speak, and go in for a* chat *with* some idle neighbor.

So, then, *we-come down to-the* class—*a very, very*-small *one*—*who-are* quick *to*-perceive *opportunities and* make-*the-most of-them*. *These-are-the* men *who-are-the* staple *of-the* race; men *who-are no* dreamers, *but* understand *what they-have to-do and do it* thoroughly; men *who* study *the* age *they* live *in, and-more especially the people their success* depends *upon*, skilfully adapting *themselves to-the* world's *greatest* needs. *They-are-the* men *who-are* proud *to* say *that-they* got *nothing but what they* toiled hard *for*. *Their*-success *was-not* attained *by* luck. *Opportunities* came *to-them as they come to all*-men; *but they--had to-be* reaped *and* garnered *in by* honest toil. *And--these-are-the* men whom shallow-pated loafers *at* street corners look *on with* envy *and suggest that "it-was* somebody's name made *him;" or it-was*-only *because-he "happened to-be* there *at-the*-time;*" or "it-was so*, then, *but--those* good old times *are* gone now." Men said similar *things of-each-other in-the* days *of* Solomon, *and-they-will go on* uttering such inanities *for all*-time. . . .

Yet *no* man *has ever* found *a short* cut *to*-Success *any* permanent good *to-him*. *There-is a* broad *and* straight *highway that* leads *to*-success *in* life; *and-though* many *think-they* can get *on to-it* some-*way up by*-means *of a short* cut *or a* bye-path, *they* generally find *in-the* end *that-they-have to* fall *in*-line *with-the* procession, *and must-be* content *to-go with-the* tail *of-it*. *As a* rule, *the* man, *be he* good *or* bad, *who* starts off *with-the* determination *to-be* rich early *in* life *is-the* one *most-*likely *to-be* disappointed.

Cause (and) effect *are what a* man *has to-*study *if-he-would-be* successful. Men *should-be* taught *to* observe nature *and* life *and to* utilize *and* elevate *what they see. Happy* inspirations *may come; but-they* need labor *to--give them-the* proper effect. *To-*succeed *in-any* enterprise needs *great strength of-character and* indomitable industry. Wise-men *must* watch, alter *or* adapt *their* conduct *according-to circumstances.*

*It-is all-very-*well *to* advocate *the* virtue *of* Consistency, *but it-*won't do *in-*Business; *it-is-rather a* sign *of* weakness *to* stick *to a* routine just *for-the* sake-*of* being consistent. *By-all-*means let-*us-have* consistent honesty *and--*industry; *but never* consistent obstinacy. *No* firm *can* flourish long *on-the* reputation *of-its* antecedents; *the* changing *wishes and-*wants *of-*customers *have to-be* met, *and-*even anticipated.

The philosophy *of-life is to-*make-*the* best *of things as--they happen,* taking-*the* good *with-the* bad, accepting *misfortune with* complacency, learning lessons *from disappointment, and* bearing humiliation *with-dignity. The* man *who-can* meet *his* troubles bravely *will* make-*the--most out-of his opportunities. It-is-not all who-can undergo and* survive-*the* scant fare *and* hard-work necessary *to-*success. *It-is* hard *to-*fight *one's way up and* make *a* fortune *out-of nothing by-way-*(of) *a* beginning; *but-that--is-the-way the* biggest fortunes *have-been* made. *It-is-the* discipline *and* hard experience *that* successful men *have-had to undergo which gives-them the* discrimination *and* tact necessary *to* decide *when to-*grasp *a great opportunity; the* faculty *of knowi*ng *how to-do-the* right *thing at-the* **right** time.

APPENDIX.

ADVANCED SPEED PRACTICE.

1. The student who desires to utilize his knowledge of Shorthand chiefly in the writing of business letters or commercial matter of various kinds has been amply catered for in the preceding pages, and if he has carefully followed the directions and faithfully worked through the exercises provided, he will now, doubtless, find himself fairly well equipped for the ordinary work of Shorthand Amanuensis or Business Correspondent. The following remarks are intended principally for those students who desire to acquire a higher rate of speed in writing than is necessary, as a general rule, for ordinary business purposes.

2. Though it is assumed that the student has by this time acquired the ability to write at a fair rate of speed, it may not be out of place to remind him that he should keep a constant and careful check upon the size and style of the outlines he employs; that he should resist the slightest tendency to "scrawl"; and that he should scrupulously avoid combinations, whether outlines of single words or of phrases, that in any way check the hand or in the least degree affect the legibility of the notes. It does not, of course, follow from this that the same size or style of outlines should or can be recommended to all writers. In this matter a good deal must be left to the individual characteristics of the writer. At the same time, regard must be paid to the experience of the fastest writers during the last seventy years; and this experience goes to prove that the use of abnormally large outlines does not make for speed. Every possible effort, therefore, should be made by the student to reproduce shorthand outlines which do not exceed the size of those given in this book.

3. It is a fact that, as a rule, hesitancy in the writing of shorthand is not merely or so much a matter of slowness of the hand as of a lack of quickness in the mind; that is to say, after a reasonable amount of practice the student is able to write quickly enough any word with the outline of which he is familiar, or the rules governing which he knows thoroughly well. It is when he has to *think* of the outline that he is lost. The conclusions are, of course, obvious: he should first of all have a perfect mastery of the rules of the system, so as to be able to apply them instantly; he should, by regular reading practice, familiarize himself with the shorthand outlines for the majority of common words; and he should supplement this by persistent exercise in writing from dictation. There is a practically unlimited supply of very suitable reading matter in shorthand characters, and it is only necessary here to refer the student to the lists at the end of the present book.

4. It should be remembered, too, that there is quite as much individuality in shorthand writing as in ordinary longhand; from which the student will see how desirable it is that he should be thoroughly familiar with his own style of shorthand notes, and should accustom himself to their peculiarities, in order that he may have no difficulty with the deciphering of his notes, even when they have been written at a high speed.

5. As regards the acquisition of a higher rate of speed, of course the best plan is to practise from actual dictation and on varied matter. Where, however, it is not possible to obtain dictation practice, very considerable progress can be made by practising writing between the lines of a widely spaced book. Increased speed, it will be found, comes almost insensibly as the writer enlarges his knowledge of outlines and becomes perfectly familiar with the commonly recurring words and phrases to be met with in general literature. It is quite possible for a

writer to cultivate a speed of 150 words a minute, using the method just referred to. Any word which occasions difficulty to the writer should be looked up, the correct outline found, and the word written out a number of times until perfect facility in writing it is secured.

6. The student should not be discouraged if at the beginning he finds himself unable to take a verbatim note of a speaker. The ability to do this depends not merely upon fast shorthand writing, but upon the power to concentrate attention upon the subject matter of the discourse as it is delivered, and to overcome the nervousness with which most young writers are troubled at the outset of their reporting practice. The note-taker must necessarily be some words behind the speaker, and until he becomes accustomed to this he is apt to become flurried when the speaker increases the pace, and so to make notes which are in parts almost illegible. This trouble, however, will disappear after a time, and the writer will soon acquire the calmness, self-possession, and confidence necessary to the successful note-taker.

7. It can scarcely be necessary in these days to impress upon the shorthand writer the importance of using a pen for note-taking. Whether from the point of view of ease of writing or of legibility, the pen is undoubtedly and immeasurably superior to the pencil. Most professional reporters use fountain pens; but for ordinary office purposes a medium pointed steel pen and the usual quality of ink will be found to answer very well.

8. As regards the paper used for note-taking, this should not be too highly-glazed. A fine, smooth surface, over which the pen glides easily, is the best. The "Fono" Series Elastic Bound Note-Books that open flat on the desk are in very general use, and can be recommended. The following advice as to turning over the leaves of the note-book has been proved to be excellent in every way:—"While writing on the upper half of the leaf,

introduce the second finger of the left hand between it and the next leaf, keeping the leaf which is being written on steady by the first finger and thumb. While writing on the lower half of the page shift the leaf by degrees till it is about half-way up the book, and at a convenient moment lift up the first finger and thumb, and the leaf will turn over almost of itself. This is the best plan when writing on a desk or table. When writing on the knee, the first finger should be introduced instead of the second, and the leaf be shifted up only about two inches. The finger should be introduced at the first pause the speaker makes, or at any other convenient opportunity that presents itself." Some shorthand writers prefer to take hold of the bottom left-hand corner of the leaf with the finger and thumb, slightly crease the paper, and on reaching the bottom line lift the page and turn it over. In any case, only one side of the note-book should be used until the end of the book is reached, when it should be turned over and the remaining blank pages used as described.

9. It is sometimes necessary for the shorthand writer to indicate a mishearing, a reference or quotation, etc., in order that he may be guided when making his transcription. The various marks employed in this connection are here described:—

MISHEARINGS, ETC.—When a word has not been heard distinctly, and the shorthand writer is uncertain whether he has written the right one or not, a circle should be drawn round the character, or a cross (×) placed under it. When the note-taker has failed to hear a word, the omission should be indicated by a caret (⋯⋀⋯) placed *under* the line. Should a portion of a sentence be so lost, the same sign should be employed, and a space left blank corresponding to the amount omitted. Or the longhand letters *n h* (*not heard*) may be written.

ERRORS.—In cases where a reporter has failed to secure a correct note of a sentence, this may be indicated by an inclined oval, thus ⌀ (*nought* or *nothing*). When it is noticed that the speaker has fallen into an error, the mark ✕ should be made on the left-hand margin of the note-book.

REFERENCE MARKS.—When verbatim notes of a speech are taken, but only a condensed report is required, a perpendicular stroke should be made in the left-hand margin of the note-book to indicate an important sentence or passage which it is desirable to incorporate in the summary. The end of a speech or the completion of a portion of a discourse may be indicated by two strokes, thus // When the reporter suspends note-taking, but the speaker proceeds, the longhand letters *c s* (*continued speaking*) may be written.

QUOTATIONS, ETC.—Quotations from well-known sources, such as the Bible or Shakspere, familiar to the reporter, need not be written fully if time presses. It will suffice to write the commencing and concluding words with quotation marks and a long dash between, thus, "*The quality of mercy ——— seasons justice.*" A long dash may be used to denote the repetition of certain words by a speaker instead of writing them each time, as in the familiar passage, "*Whatsoever things are true, ——— honest, ——— just,*" etc.

EXAMINATION OF WITNESSES. — In reporting the examination of witnesses in questions and answers, the name of each witness should be written in longhand. The name of the examiner may be written in shorthand before the first question. If the judge, or other person, intervenes with questions during the examination, his name must be written before the first question; it need not be repeated, but care must be taken to write the name of the original examiner when he resumes his questions. Various methods may be employed for dividing questions from answers, and the answer from the succeeding question, but, whatever plan is employed, it should be one which is absolutely distinctive. When a document is put in, write *document* between large parentheses, thus (L) When a document is put in and read, write (L)

APPLAUSE, DISSENT, ETC. — The following words, descriptive of the approbation or dissent of an audience, should be enclosed by the reporter within large parentheses:— *hear*, *hear, hear*, *no*, *no*, *no*, *sensation*, *applause*, *chair*, *cheers*, *laughter*, *uproar*, *hisses*. The adjective, or adjectives, descriptive of the kind of applause must be written after the first word. For example, what would be described as *loud and continued applause* would be written _____ in reporting, for the note-taker would not know that the applause was continued till it had lasted for some time.

10. In sermon reporting the Book or Epistle, the Chapter, and the Verse in quotations from the Bible may be indicated as follows:—Place the figure for the Book or Epistle in the first position; for the Chapter in the second position; and for the Verse in the third position, thus, 2 6 5 1 By this method, the book, chapter, and verse may be written in any order by means of figures only, without danger of ambiguity.

LAW PHRASES.

The following lists of commonly recurring law phrases will be found useful to writers who have to deal with legal matter.

Actual damage
affidavit and order
articles of agreement
as to the matters
as to these matters
as to those matters
Bankruptcy Court
before him
before me
being duly sworn
beneficial estate
beneficial interest
bill of sale
breach of promise of marriage
by this action
by this court
called for the defendant
called for the plaintiff
called in is own behalf

Central Criminal Court
circumstantial evidence
Circuit Court
City Court
common jury
common law
County Clerk
County Court
County Treasurer
counsel for the defense
counsel for the defendant
counsel for the plaintiff
counsel for the prisoner
counsel for the prosecution
Court of Appeals
Court of Bankruptcy
Court of Claims
Court of Equity
Court of General Sessions
Court of Justice
Court of Record

Court of Special Sessions
criminal jurisprudence
cross examination
deed of settlement
deed of trust
defendant's testimony
direct evidence
direct examination
District Attorney
District Court
do you mean to say
documentary evidence
Ecclesiastical Court
employer's liability
equity of redemption
Federal Court
fee simple
fiduciary capacity
final decree
for defendant
for plaintiff

for this action
for this court
general term
gentlemen of the jury
goods and chattels
government securities
grand jury
gross receipts
Habeas Corpus
heirs, executors, administrators *and* assigns
heirs, executors, administrators *or* assigns
If Your Honor please
in this action
in this court
in witness whereof
interlocutory decree
international law
joint stock
joint stock company
judicial sale
judgment for plaintiff

LAW PHRASES.

- judgment for defendant
- justice of the peace
- last will and testament
- learned counsel for the defense
- learned counsel for the defendant
- learned counsel for the plaintiff
- learned counsel for the prisoner
- learned counsel for the prosecution
- learned judge
- legal estate
- letters of administration
- letters patent
- letters testamentary
- life estate
- malice prepense
- manslaughter
- marine insurance
- may it please the court
- may it please Your Honor
- memorandum of agreement
- motion to dismiss
- motion granted
- motion denied
- Municipal Court
- my learned friend
- next of kin
- no, sir
- notary public
- objection sustained
- objected to by plaintiff
- objected to by defendant
- offered in evidence
- official receiver
- of this action
- of this agreement
- of this court
- on the other side of the case
- on the following grounds
- originating summons
- particulars of our claim
- particulars of your claim
- Patent office
- peculiar circumstances of the case

penal offense
personal estate
petit jury
plaintiff's case
plaintiff's counsel
plaintiff's testimony
plaintiff's witnesses
Police Court
power of attorney
preliminary injunction
prisoner at the bar
quit claim
real estate
rebutting testimony
re-cross examination
reversionary interest
right of way
special jury
special license
state whether or not
summary proceedings
Superior Court

Supreme Court
Surrogate Court
sworn and examined
tax deed
that this action
that this court
testimony of the defendant
testimony of the plaintiff
trust funds
under the circumstances of the case
verdict for the defendant
verdict for the plaintiff
verdict for the jury
voluntary conveyance
Ward of the Court
warrant of attorney
what is your business
where do you reside
where is your place of business
will and testament
without prejudice
wrongful possession
yes, sir
your Honor

LEGAL CORRESPONDENCE.
(1.)

Mr. Edward Richmond,
   St. Louis, Mo.

Dear-Sir:

In-reply-*to-your*-letter *of* Dec. 22, requesting *information in*-regard-*to-the* status *of-the* case *of* Clara Kyle vs. Joseph Kyle, *I*-beg-*to*-inform-*you that*, pending-*the* trial *for* separation, *an* order *of* arrest *has-been* issued, *and-the defendant* placed *in* custody under $500 bail. Application *for a* writ *of* habeas-corpus *has-been*-made *to* Justice Scott.

Respectfully,

[73

(2.)

Mr. Matthew Jennings,
   Albany, *N. Y.*

Dear-Sir:

Some-time-*ago I* addressed *a* letter *to-your*-place *of* business regarding *a* bill *of* $640, *which-is* due *the* Elite Printing Company. *My* collector *informs me that your* office *at* 240 Main Street *has-been* closed *for over a* month. *In*-order-*that-you* shall-not-be-able-*to*-claim *that-you did- -not* receive due *and* seasonable notice, *I-have* instructed *that-this* be served *on-you* personally. *I-shall* wait three- -days before taking legal-proceedings *to* enforce payment.

Yours-truly,

[93

(3.)

Mr. Geo. H. Day,
   40 Wall Street,
      New York City.

Dear-Sir:

An account against *you for* personal services rendered, amounting *to* $450 *has-been* placed *in-my hands for* collection *by Mr.* James Fraser. Unless payment *of-this*-account *is* made *by* Thursday, January 8, *I-shall--sue. As-the* result *of-*such *a* suit *would-be an* award *of* costs against *you* besides-*the* amount *of-the* bill, *I-*trust *you-will-see-the* advisability *of* settling before-*the* date mentioned.

Respectfully,

[84

(4.)

Mr. Clarence F. Walker,
    Pittsburg, Pa.
Dear-Sir:

*Have-*just-received *your certificate of* incorporation *from-the* Secretary-*of-*State. *I* hasten *to* transmit *it to--you,* regretting *that, owing to-the* fact *that-the* objects *of--your* association conflict *somewhat with-the* insurance law, *and* also *because-the* justices *of-the* Supreme-Court are *very* busy *at-*present, *I-was-*unable *to* obtain *it* sooner. *As-it-is,* papers *had to-be* re-drafted three-times, once *owing to-the* careless signatures *of-the* incorporators, *and* twice *on-*account *of-the* reasons stated *above*.

You-will receive *a certificate of* incorporation *in* (a) -few-days.

Very-truly-yours,

[108

(5.)

Mr. Robert Jones,
    Minneapolis, Minn.
Dear-Sir:

We-beg-*to*-inform-*you that-we-are* owners *of United--States* letters patent *No.* 645,432, dated Dec. 6, 1906, *and* granted *upon-the* invention *of* Arthur Wells *for Improvement in* Bicycle Pedals. Prior *to-the* purchase *of-this* patent, *we-had-the* question *of-its* validity passed upon, *and-on-the* favorable report made *to-us* we purchased *the* patent. *Other* attorneys besides *those-who* acted *for-us* have examined *the* patent *and-we-are-in-*

-possession *of-their* favorable reports *or of* copies *of--them*. Since-*we* acquired-*the* title *of-the* patent, *we--have*-taken steps *to*-protect *our* exclusive right *as-to--the* invention, *and are-now* prosecuting suits against infringers.

As you doubtless *know, or will-be* advised *by your* counsel, *everyone who manufactures,* uses *or* sells bicycle pedals embodying-*the* invention *of-the* Wells patent *is an* infringer *and-is* accountable *to-us for-his* profits *as--well-as for our* damages *by*-reason *of*-loss *of-trade*.

Recently *it-has-been* brought *to-our* attention *that-you--are* dealing *in* bicycle pedals *which* infringe *upon this* patent. *We* desire *to-give-you this* formal notice *of-our* rights *in-the*-premises, *and to* caution *you to* cease *at--once from* further infringement *upon-the* Wells patent. *Your* failure *to* cease *from* infringement *will of*-course make-*you* liable *to-us for* future damages *and*-profits, *as--well-as for-those-which-have* already accrued *from-your* infringement.

Yours-very-truly,

(6.) [254

Mr. J. L. Gibbons,
    Milwaukee, Wis.
Dear-Sir:

Mr. Clarke *informed me that-the* jury rendered judgment *in-our* case *on*-Thursday last. Now, *if-the-amount of-the* judgment *is-not* paid, *you-will* kindly *send me a* transcript *of-the* judgment, *and-I-can* collect *the* same here.

Permit *me to*-congratulate *you upon-the* good work *which* led *to-the* successful termination *of-this*-case.

Awaiting *your*-reply *and-thank*ing *you for* past favors, *I*-remain,

Very-truly-yours,

[82

(7.)

Mr. Henry Morris,
> Pittsburg, Pa.

Dear-Sir:

Received *this*-day *a* notice *of* appearance *in-your* -case against *Mr.* Bell. *He*-appears *on* behalf *of* Messrs. Candler & Jay, *of* 48 Broadway, *who-are-*considered *first*-rate specialists *in* defending slander *and* libel suits. *The* appearance *in-the* Milton suit *is* due *not*-later-than Monday *next, and-I-will-be-able-to-tell-you by-that-*time *who-his* attorneys *will-be in-the* suit. *As-the-*cases now stand *I-will-have to-*employ further-labor *and* time *in-this-* -matter, *and-in-*view *of-this and-the* fact *that-you-are-in a* steady position now, *I*-request *that-you*-make some payment towards-*the balance of-my* fee, amounting *to* $40, some-time *next-*week.   *Yours-truly,*   [131

(8.)

Mr. Ralph Nelson,
> Philadelphia, Pa.

Dear-Sir:

*I-am-in-*receipt-*of-your-*letter dated Dec. 10. *The* partnership suit *is* proceeding *very-*slowly *owing to a* dispute between Wilson *and* Yates.

*I-am-*sorry *to* note *what you* say about *your* marriage. *If* retained, *I-will* protect *your* interests *the* best *I-can in-the-*matter. *From-the* facts stated, *I-believe-that-you* -*could* sue *for* annulment *of-the* marriage *on-the* theory *of-*fraud.

If-your wife *should* sue, *the* court *is* likely *to* allow alimony *and* counsel fee.   *Yours-truly,*   [94

(9.)

Secretary-*of-*State,
> Capitol, Albany, *N. Y.*

*Dear-*Sir:

Enclosed-please-find original *and* copy *of-certificate of* incorporation *of-the* American Automobile-Company.

I-have by-this mail *sent-the* State Treasurer *the* sum *of* $50, *being-the* statutory tax *on-the* capital stock *of* $60,000. Kindly file *the* original *and* please *to-*return-*the* copy *to-me with your usual* endorsements *as-to-the* full requirements *of-the* law, *so-that I-may* file *the* same *in-the* County--Clerk's Office. *I* also enclose *my* check for $25 *for* filing and recording certified copy.

*Yours-very-tru*ly, [98

(10.)

Lawrence Coal-Company,
    Coal *Yards*, North River,
        New York.

Gentlemen:

Mr. Martin Reeves *has* placed *his* claim *for an* injury *to his* carriage caused *by-your* truck *No.* 84 *on-the* 25th day *of* May, 1913, *at* Chatham Square, *New-York* City, *in-my hands for professional* attention.

I personally rode *in-the* carriage *with Mr.* Reeves *when--the* damage *was-done, and-there-is-no-*question *that your* driver *was in* fault *and-that-you-are* liable.

A prompt settlement *will* save *you* time, trouble, *and--the* expense *of a* law-suit. Please-let-*me* hear *from-you at*-once.

Yours-truly, [102

(11.)

Mr. Fred W. Lawrence,
    49 Broadway, Brooklyn, *N. Y.*

*Dear-*Sir:

The examination *of-the* directors *of-the* Long Island *Electric-*Company *is* set *for* to-morrow, Wednesday, May 6, 1914, *at-the* office *of* Charles A. Townsend, *in* Long Island City.

*I-*expect *that-it-will-be-*necessary *for-me to-*refer *to-the* books *of-the* corporation, *and-have-sent to Mr.* B. Bartram's office *for-them. I-am-informed by Mr.* Dodd *that-the* books *are at-your* office, *and-therefore* request *you to* kindly let *the* bearer *have-them to-*produce *on behalf of Mr.* B. Bartram *at-the* examination.

Thanking *you in-*advance, *I-*am,
         Yours-respectfully,   [111

(12.)

Mr. Arthur D. Pindar,
  Holland House, Boston, Mass.
*Dear-*Sir:

*My-*client, *Mr.* John Edward Gates, *has* placed *a* draft *for* twenty pounds, *on the* London Joint-Stock--Bank Limited, *and* returned *by-them* N. G., *in-my hands for professional* attention. *When my representative called at-your* office *he-was* told *that-you-were* out-*of-*town.

Unless *you call* here *on or* before Thursday *next and* pay *the* same *I-will-have to-*take further steps *in-the--matter and see to-it that-you-are* found. *Your* prompt--attention *will* save *you* time, trouble *and* expense. Please-let-*me* hear *from-you at-*once.
         Yours-truly,   [109

(13.)

Mr. William Sanders,
  438 Court Street, Brooklyn, N. Y.
*Dear-*Sir:

A claim *has this-*day *been* placed *in-my hands* against *you* amounting *to-the-*sum *of* fifty *dollars, which-*sum *is* due *my-*client, *Mr.* Robinson, *and-*unless *I* receive check *for-the above* amount, *at-my* office, *above* address, **on or** before-*the* 15th instant, *I-shall-be-*compelled *to immediately* institute legal-proceedings against *you for-the* recovery *of* said amount *and* costs.

Trusting *you-will-take-the* wiser course *of* paying *this* small amount, thereby avoiding *the* trouble *and* expense *of* unnecessary litigation, *I-*remain,
         Yours-truly,   [102

(14.)

Messrs. Arnold Hunt & Co.,
    Chicago, Ill.
Gentlemen:

Word has reached *me that your* client *or an* agent *of--your* client *in-the above* action *has* approached *the plaintiff with a* view *towards-the* settlement *of-the* same.

I merely *wish to* notify *you that any*-further attempt *to* settle-(the)-matter *in-my* absence *will-be* effectually frustrated *by-me, as* such conduct is, *to say-the* least, uncalled *for,* inasmuch *as I-have-been and* shall at-all--times *be will*ing *to* entertain *any* proposition *of* settlement made *in* good faith. *If-you* desire *to-do-so,* kindly communicate *with me.*

*Yours-very-tru*ly,
[106

(15.)

Messrs. B. & J. Rollins,
    San-Francisco, Cal.
Gentlemen:

I write *you on behalf of-my-*clients, *The* Progressive Cycle *and* Automobile Supply-Company, *who-were* threatened *with* suit *for* damages *for* injuries sustained *by-*reason *of-*certain bicycle forks *not* braced.

*My-*clients claim *that said* forks *were* supplied *by-you, and* desire *that I* obtain *from-you in* writing *a* statement *to-the* effect *that-you-will* hold *them* harmless *from any* kind *and-all* damages *which they-may-be called-upon to* pay *by-*reason *of-the defective* bicycle forks heretofore supplied *by-you.*

Immediately upon receipt *of-said* agreement *they-will send you* check *in* full settlement *of-their-*account. Please--let-*me* hear *from-you.*

*Yours-very-tru*ly,
[123

(16.)

Mr. L. S. Wilson,
  Oakland, Cal.

Dear-Sir:

I-am-in-receipt-*of-your*-favor *of* June 7 *in*-regard--*to-the*-case *of* Mannings vs. Williams being set *down for* trial *for* June 23 instead-*of* June 25, 1914. *I-would-be*-greatly obliged-*to-you if-it could-be sent down for* trial *for any other*-day than June 25th, *because on-that-day it-is-impossible for-me to-be in* Court, *owing to-the* fact *that I-have* two other matters *which-are* set *down for-the*-same day *in* Special-Term *of-the* Supreme-Court, King's County.

I therefore enclose *you* herewith *a* stipulation setting *the* case *over to any other*-day *in* June *after-the* 25th. *You--may* fill *in-the* date *and* return *one* copy *of-the* stipulation.

Thanking *you in*-advance, *I*-am,

Yours-truly, [143

(17.)

Mr. B. C. Price,
  Ridgway, Pa.

Dear-Sir:

Referring *to-the within* claim *from Mr*. Johnson relative *to* damage *to* chest, *it-would* appear *that* baggage master George Simpson *has no* record *of-this* chest *as* being *in* bad order *when delivered at-your* station. Please interview *him on-this-subject and* also ask *him if-he-can* make affidavit *that no* articles *were* lost *out-of it while in-his--*charge. *I*-presume *it-would-be* well *for-you* to see-*the* party *and-have-the* chest repaired, *but if no* articles *were* lost *at-your* station, *and* Simpson says none *were* lost *while in-his*-charge, *we would be* averse *to* entertaining *any* claim *for* missing articles, *the* loss *of-which may-have* occurred *after-the* chest left *our* hands.

Yours-very-truly, [135

(18.)

Mr. Joseph H. Curtis,
    Newark, N. J.
*Dear-*Sir:

Mr. Frank Wells *has this-*day *called on-me informing me of-the* fact *that-you would* like *to* consult *me in-*regard-*-to-the-*case *of* Wells against Walsh, *and-I-am-very-much interested in-the* result *of-this-*case. *I would-be-*pleased *to-have-you call at-my* office *any* afternoon except Saturday before-*the* 31st *inst., if-this-is-*convenient, *and-we-can* then *go over all-the* facts relative *to-this-case.*

Yours-respectfully, [89

(19.)

Mr. G. F. Mills,
    Matawan, N. J.
*Dear-*Sir:

I return herewith letter received, dated *the* 18th *inst., from Mr.* Smith addressed *to-you, which-was sent me with yours of-*May 19, *and-after* taking *the* matter *up with* our General-Manager *I-have* written *a* letter *as* per copy attached, giving *the* approval *of-this* company *to-the* proposition *as* desired. *You-will* note-*that-it-will-be-*necessary *for-the-*persons desiring *this* privilege *to-*sign *one-of-our regular* agreements, *and-I would-be-*glad *if-you* would arrange *to-have-this* agreement properly prepared *in-the* usual way *and-after* same *has-been* signed *have-it* forwarded *to-the* Real-Estate-Department *for* execution *and* record.

Very-truly-yours, [124

(20.)

Mr. B. J. Wright,
    741 Broadway, Portland, Oregon.
*Dear-*Sir:

I wrote *you on* July 2 last advising *you that-the* decree *in-the* Ward Estate matter *has-been* signed *by* Surrogate Fitzgerald, *and* requesting *you to-*send *me* motion papers ordering *the* City Chamberlain *to-*turn *over-the balance in-his-hands to-you or-the* Administratrix *and-that I would give-the-*matter *immediate-*attention, *but have-*received *no* reply. Please send *on-the* papers *and let-us* get *this-*matter fixed *up, as you* seem *to-have-been very* anxious *to-have-the-*matter disposed *of when* here.

Yours-truly,   [103

(21.)

Mr. Frank L. Mayhew,
    Kingston, N. Y.

*Dear-*Sir:

*My-*clients, The Manhattan Fixture-Company, *have-placed a* claim secured *by* chattel *mortgage, in-my hands for-*attention, *for-your* failure *to* pay *this* month's instalment *when* due. They claim *that-they-have* reduced *the* instalment from $45 to $35 *on-your* express promise *that-you would* meet *the* payments promptly.

Unless *I-*receive settlement *of-this* month's payment *on or* before Friday, September 13, 1914, *I-will-*place-*the* mortgage *in the hands of a* City Marshal *for* foreclosure. Your prompt-attention *will* save *you* considerable time, trouble *and* expense.

Yours-truly,   [103

(22.)

Messrs. Walker & Morris,
    Pittsburg, Pa.

Gentlemen:

Enclosed-please-find *two* claims *of-my-*client, G. R. Henry, *one* amounting *to* $36.95 *and-the-other to* $45.55, *for* collection. *I* also enclose *a* letter *sent to-me by-the* latter, L. Crane, claiming *an* allowance *for* damaged goods. *The* goods were shipped *to-him on* August 22, *and as-he* claimed some damages *an* allowance *of* $4 *was* credited *to-him. At-that-*time *this-was satisfactory* to-him, *but* now *that my*-client insists *on* payment, *he* claims *a* further concession, *for*-the-purpose-of delay.

Please *give these*-matters *your*-attention, *and-after* collecting remit *to-me the* proceeds.   *Yours-truly,*   [113

(23.)

The B. H. Hall Company,
    Trenton, N. J.
Gentlemen:

Your-favor *of*-March 15 received. *In*-answer *will--say that* being careful *in* drawing papers, *I-do-not-think I* omitted *the* fire insurance clause *in mortgage* executed *by-the.* Metropolitan Sign-Company *to-you. At-any*-rate *an inspection of-the mortgage sent to-you with my*-letter *of*-May 21 *will* disclose matters.

In-reference-*to-the* chances *of* collecting *on-the* two notes *in-my hands, I*-beg *to*-refer *to-my*-letter *of-the* 14th *in-which I*-said *that Mr.* Meyer *called* here *and--claimed that-the* company *is* unable *to-meet* its obligations.

Mr. Martin promised *to-call* here *in a* day *or* two *and--I-will* talk-*the*-matter *over with him.*

        Yours-respectfully,   [131

(24.)

Mr. Martin Decker,
    Brooklyn, *N. Y.*
Dear-Sir:

Your postal *of-the* 8th *inst.* received *and* contents noted. *In*-reply *I would*-say *that-the*-motion *in-your--case was-not* argued *on*-Monday *for-the* reasons *which I* stated *to-you when you*-were *at-my* office *on*-Saturday last. *It-was* set *down for* argument *for* Monday, August 20, *when-it-will* positively be disposed *of.*

. *I* spoke *to-the* lawyer *in*-regard-*to a* settlement, *but-we* arrived *at no* definite conclusion. *There-will* positively be *no*-further adjournments *in-the-matter, and-it-will-be* disposed *of on-the* 20th.   *Yours-very-truly,*   [107

(25.)

Mr. G. D. Moffat,
     Richmond, Va.
Dear-Sir:

My-client, *Mr.* James E. Sheldon, consulted *with me in* reference-*to* some sheds erected *in yard and above building, No.* 47 East 10th Street, *and-informs me that--it-is your* intention *to* tear *the* same *down upon your* removal. *I-have* advised *Mr.* Sheldon *that as-these* sheds *have-not-been* attached *to-the* realty, *they-have become* part *of*-such, *and are his* absolute property, *and cannot-be* removed *by the* tenants except *at-their-own* peril. '*You--will-therefore take*-notice *that my*-client intends *to* sue *should you* detach *the* same *from-the* realty.

By giving *this*-matter *your*-attention, *you-will* save *yourself time, trouble* and expense *of a* law-suit.
                                            Yours-truly,   [126

(26.)

Mr. S. J. Carpenter,
     Deland, Fla.
Dear-Sir:

I-find *in* looking *over-my* papers *this*-day *that-the* first *meeting of-the* creditors *of* Samuel J. Conklin, Bankrupt, *and-the meeting of-the* creditors of Donnalson & Company, Bankrupts, *cannot-be* held to-morrow *as* originally agreed *upon, but I-have* prepared *for-the first meeting in-the*-matter *of* John Lowell, Bankrupt, *and-the meeting of-the* creditors *of* Lewis J. Monroe, Bankrupt, *which--will-be* held *at-my* offices *to*-morrow *at* 2 o'clock *in-the* afternoon.

I-have-not as yet advertised *in-the* Samuel J. Conklin *and-the* Donnalson & Company bankruptcies, *and-it-will--be-impossible for-me to-have-the* meetings *in-those*-matters before-*the* 20th *or* 23rd *of next*-month, *which-is-the very--best I-can-do under-the-circumstances.*
                                            Yours-very-truly,   [141

(27.)

Messrs. Wilcox & Greene,
    Alpena, Mich.
Gentlemen:

For-the third-time *we-call-your*-attention *to-the* fact *that-as* attorneys *for-the* Stearns & Eagan Company *we--have a* claim against *you for* $500, *which-must*-now be paid, *or in-the* alternative, *we*-demand *that-the* "Little Masterpieces" be returned *to-us.*

The books *do-not* become *your* property until fully paid *for, and-as you have thus* far ignored *our* courteous requests *for*-payment, *we*-demand *the-immediate* payment *or* return *of-our* books. *If-you* continue *to* show *no* disposition *to* settle *with-us we-shall-be*-obliged *to*-take legal action *to* obtain *our* rights *in-the*-matter. *We-have this*-day drawn *on-you at*-sight. *If-the*-draft *is-not* honored *at-once we-shall* begin action. *Yours-very-truly,*   [136

(28.)

The Owl Brewing Company,
    New Orleans, La.
Gentlemen:

Your-favor *of-the* 7th *inst. is* received *in*-regard-*to a* certain cash register *and* glass case removed *from No.* 43 East 31st Street *which-you* claim *as your* property. *In*-reply *would*-say *that if-you-can give me* proof *of-the* fact *that-the* cash register *and-the* glass case *which-were* removed *from* said premises belong *to-you or that-you--are*-entitled *to-the* possession *of*-same, *I would-be*-pleased *to see that-they are* returned *to-you. If*-convenient *you--may-have one-of-your representatives* call *at-my* office *any* afternoon except Saturday *with* proofs *of* ownership, etc., *and-this*-matter *will-be* properly disposed *of without any*-further delay.

Hoping same *is* satisfactory, *I*-am,
                    Yours-very-truly,   [134

(29.)

Messrs. Campbell & Reay,
    Detroit, Mich.

Gentlemen:

A few-days since *we* wrote *you that as* attorneys *for--the* Bennett & Smith-Company *we* hold *a* claim against *you for* $7.50, *and-as-this-is* such *a* small matter *we-must* insist *upon-your* payment *without* further delay. *As you well-know, you have-no* title *to-the* books until *you have* paid *all of-the* instalments, *and-therefore we-must-have* either-*the* books *or-the* money.

We-trust *that-you-will-see-the* advisability *of* settling *without-the* expense attached *to-our usual* process *for-the* recovery *of-such*-accounts. *Our instructions are to* push *this*-matter.   *Yours-very-truly,*   [112

(30.)

Messrs. William Meeker & Co.,
    Roseville, N. J.

Gentlemen:

Enclosed-please find *our* standard advertising rule, *which-is* guaranteed *to-be* absolutely correct, *and which--we*-trust *may-be of*-some use *to-you in-your* business.

Thinking you, like many *other* publishers, *may-have on-your* books *a* number *of* subscribers *and* advertisers *who-have* made *no* response *to-your*-request *for* settlement, *we-beg-to-call-your*-attention *to*-some points *of-our* business. *Our* eight *years'* experience *in-this* business, confining ourselves strictly *to* publishers' accounts, *together with-the* fact *that-we-are*-now collecting 90% *of--*lists handled *by us*—collecting *during-the year* 1906 over $1,000,000 *for* publishers—*is* some evidence *of-the* fact *that-we-can, and do,* get-*the* money. *Our* terms *are* commission only *on-the* amounts collected. *Should you* desire further *information or particulars* regarding *our* methods, *on* receipt *of-the* enclosed postal card *our representative will-call on-you.*

Awaiting *your*-favors, *we-*are, *Respectfully-yours,*   [166

(31.)

Mr. William H. Clarke,
    Memphis, Tenn.

Dear-Sir:

I-called at-the Jefferson Market Police-Court *yester-day* afternoon *very-shortly after-you* left, *and-I-was informed by-the* Magistrate then presiding *there that-he* gave *you* time until Tuesday morning *to* pay *up, and* failing *this that-he-would* issue warrant.

Now *I-wish to* say *that I-expect-you at-my* office *not--later-than* 10:30 o'clock Tuesday-morning, *the* 3d day *of* August, *and-if-you do-not* call *at-that-*time, *I-shall-be--obliged to-take* further steps *as* indicated *by-the justice of* Jefferson Market Police-Court. *If-it-had-not-been for--the* fact *of Mr.* John's leniency *towards you, he-would--have* pressed *the* charges *as-he-was told to-do by-the* judge, *but he-is too-much of a gentleman to-*take such action *if-the* accused *is* willing *to-*make *an* amicable-arrangement. *I* would *therefore* say *that-it-is for-your-own good not to--*cause *any-*further trouble *in-the-*matter, *and-to-call at-my* office *at-the* time named. *I-*remain,

                    Yours-truly,   [185

(32.)

Mr. N. M. Lowe,
    Macon, Ga.

Dear-Sir:

I-have looked *up-the* pleadings *in-the above* case, *and--*find *that* Judge Blanchard vacated *the* injunction *on--the original* papers. *It-may-be* possible *to-*move *for--*another injunction *on* new affidavits, *and-I-will* let *you* know *as-*soon-*as I* look *up* decisions *in* similar cases.

From an inspection of-the affidavits submitted pro *and* con, *I-*am satisfied *that if any* damages *can-be* recovered *from Mr.* Robinson *at-all by-*reason *of-the* injunction, *they-will-be of a* limited *nature.*

                    Yours-respectfully,   [96

(33.)

Mr. William Love,
Philadelphia, Pa.

Dear-Sir:

Referring-*to-your*-favor *of* a-few-days-*ago* in-regard--*to-the* leasing *of* land *which-we* bought *from* Messrs. Green & Co. *several years-ago, we would*-say *that-we-will* rent *this* property *to-you on-the* conditions printed *in-our regular* agreement, copy *of-which-is* attached *for-your information*. As, however, you desire some slight change *in-this* agreement, *we-are* willing *to* comply *with your suggestions and to*-make same *by an exchange of*-letters *to-be* attached *to-the* agreement, *but* only *on-the* following condition, namely, *that on* ten days' notice *this special* agreement *may-be* terminated *and-that-the regular* agreement *shall* then *be in* full effect. *We-shall of*-course *try to* accommodate *you as*-far-*as we-can in-this*-matter, and--*will if*-possible *give you* ample notice *of-the* termination *of-this* lease, *but it-must-be* understood that *if-we*-find *it* necessary *to*-take-*the* property *for our*-own use, *that* ten days' notice *is* all *that-will-be* demanded *by-you*. The rental *of-the* land *is* already fixed *upon and-is* shown *in-our regular* agreement attached. *If-these* details *are satisfactory to-you will-you* kindly *acknowledge* receipt *of-this*-letter *which together with your*-reply *will* then be--made *a* part *of-the original* contract.

Yours-very-truly, [234

(34.)

Mr. G. F. Hayward,
Orange St., Riverdale, N. J.

Dear-Sir:

In-reply-*to-yours of* Nov. 2, receipt *of-which has* previously *been acknowledged, and-in-which-you* ask *my* views, etc., *I*-beg leave *to* say *that-the* fact *that no two representatives of*-either *of-the* parties *to-the* contract *in*-regard-*to-the*-leasing *of*-land *have ever been able to* -agree makes-*it a subject for* constant *controversy*. Taking- -*the* question *as a* whole, *however, I-think-it-can* safely *be* assumed *that-it-was* intended *to* insure *our* company against *the establishment of* excessive charges *on* business *over-that* part *of-the* line used *as a* connecting branch, *but I-think-it-should* preserve *to-it all-the*-privileges *it-* -*has ever had through-the* ownership *of-the* entire line *for*-its business just *the* same *as-if-the* agreement *for the* joint use *had-not-been* made. The clause referred *to* covers *all* points *in-the* local territory *together with-the* roads named, *and it-would* appear *to-be sufficiently* clear, *I-think, that-* -*these* rates *should-be* revised *from*-time-*to*-time *as* changes *are* contemplated. *I-can, therefore,* reach *no other* conclusion than *that-the* position taken *in-the*-matter *is-the* correct *one. I*-am,

*Yours-very-tru*ly, [218

(35.)

Mr. W. T. Haring,
    Newark, N. J.

Dear-Sir:

I should-be-pleased *to-call-upon you and* explain *how I-have* successfully *established* law departments *in-the-* -*places of* business *of-my*-clients, whereby *all-their* legal matters, local *and out-of* town collections, receive better attention *at a* smaller cost than *by* giving *them to a* lawyer *or a* collection agency.

Your legal matters, *by-my* system, *are under your* personal control, *and* managed *by-my* devoting *several hours or more a* week *at-your* place *of* business. *I-will* furnish *the very*-best references *if* desired, *and-will* agree *to-make* no charge unless *I-can* save *you some-money. I*-am,

Yours-respectfully, [117

(36.)

Mr. D. A. Reed,
    Cincinnati, Ohio.
Dear-Sir:

I-have recently resigned *from-the* U. S. Copyright Office *after an* experience *there of*-several *years.*

As you called *on-me,* whilst *there, and* consulted *me in*-regard-*to* copyright business, *I*-take-*this opportunity to* advise *you that I-am*-prepared *to*-render services *in- -all*-matters pertaining *to*-copyright registrations, also *as to* legal questions, involving *the* validity *and* infringement *of*-copyrights.

Yours-very-truly, [76

(37.)

Mr. John Peters,
    New Orleans, La.
Dear-Sir:

Your name appears *as one of-the* creditors *of-the* Southern Bookstore-Company. *The* Receivers *are about to* file *their first* account *and* make *immediate* distribution. Please, *therefore, send* properly proven account *to-the* Receivers, 210 Main Street, *by*-return mail. *The* proof *of*-claim *should-be in-the* form *usual in* bankruptcy cases.

This-notice *is sent to all* known creditors, *whether represented by* attorneys *or* otherwise. *If-you-are* represented *by* counsel, please-forward *this*-notice *to-him immediately, so-that-he-may* prepare *the* proofs.

From present-*information, the* Receivers hope *to* pay a *first* dividend *of* 80%.

Yours-very-truly, [111

INDEX.

The figures refer to the paragraphs, except where the page is mentioned.

Acknowledgment	page 84
-ality, -arity, etc.	141
Alternative forms for *fl, fr*, etc.	64 to 66
Appendix	pages 209 to 236
Applause, Dissent, etc., Signs for	page 214
Arrange-d-ment, expressed by intersection	150
Aspirate, The; upward and downward *H*	15, 88
,, ,, added to *w*	84
,, ,, dot *h*	90
,, ,, tick *h*	89
Attention expressed by intersection	150
Authority ,, ,, ,,	150
B added to *m*	84
Bank expressed by intersection	150
Business Correspondence	pages 195 to 203
Capitals	8
Circle *s* and *z*	32 to 37
Circle *s* added to *shun* hook	81, 82
,, ,, used instead of *st* loop in phrases	48
Circles and loops prefixed to initial hooks	67 to 69
,, ,, ,, added to final hooks	76, 77
,, *sw* and *ss*	45 to 48
,, *s, sw*, and *ss* in phrasing	48
Cities, Fifty principal	179
Company expressed by intersection	150
Compound words	149
Con-, com-, cog-, cum, Prefixes	132, 133
,, Prefix, omitted in phrases	page 142
Consonants	2, 10, 14
,, Joining of	3, 10, 16
,, Half-length	98 to 107
,, Double-length	108 to 116
,, Double	58 to 65
,, ,, Names of	60
,, ,, Compound	84 to 87
,, ,, ,, Vocalization of	85 to 87
,, Table of Single and Double	page 190
Contractions and Grammalogs, List of	pages 173 to 178
,, Alphabetical list of	pages 184 to 188
,, for States and Territories	page 178
D indicated by Halving Principle	98 to 107, 114, 119

D, half-sized, when disjoined	99
Department expressed by intersection	150
Diphonic Signs	122 to 124
Diphthongs	24
,, Places of	25 to 27
,, Joined	28
,, *w* and *y* series	125 to 130
Distinguishing Vowels	151
Doubling Principle	108 to 116
Dr indicated by Doubling Principle	108, 109, 112 to 115
Enter-, Prefix	134
-er added to *mpr*, *ng-gr*	110
Errors	page 213
Examination of Witnesses	page 213
F and *N* hooks	70 to 74
Figures	148
Fl, *fr*, etc. Alternative forms for	64 to 66
-fulness, Termination	146
G, Omission of	147
-gr added to *ng*	110
Grammalog defined	9
Grammalogs alphabetically arranged	pages 181 to 183
,, and Contractions, List of	pages 173 to 178
Gw, Compound Consonant	84
Halving Principle	98 to 107, 114, 119
Here, Compounds of	149
-ility, *-arity*, etc.	141
In-, Contraction for prefix	137, 138
-ing, Suffix	140
Initial hooks to straight strokes	58, 59
,, ,, ,, curves	61 to 66
Inter-, *intro-*, Prefixes	134
Intersections	150
It indicated by Halving Principle	103
Journal expressed by intersection	150
K, Omission of	147
kr added to *ng*	110
Kw, Compound Consonant	84
L, Double-length, standing alone	113
,, Hook, to curved consonants	61
,, ,, straight ,,	58
,, hooked initially	84
,, Stroke, joined to circle and curve	38
,, Upward and Downward	38, 91 to 94
Law Phrases	pages 215 to 218

INDEX. 239

Legal Correspondence	pages 219 to 236
-lessness, Termination	146
-logical	141
-lousness	146
Logogram defined	9
Logogram *all*, Joined	44
Loops *st* and *str*	40 to 42
Lr, Compound Consonant	84
,, ,, ,, cannot be halved	106
,, ,, ,, when to use	95
-ly, Suffix	144
Magna-i-e, Prefix	135
Medial circle for *s* only	76
-ment, Suffix	142
-mental-ity, Suffixes	143
Mishearings, etc.	page 212
Mp, Compound Consonant	84
,, ,, ,, hooked initially	84
,, ,, ,, Double-length	110
,, ,, ,, Half-length	106
N and *F* hooks	70 to 74
Negative prefixes	139
Ng hooked	63, 110
,, Double-length	110
,, Half-length	106
Not expressed by Halving Principle	103
ns, nss, nst, nstr, after a curve	78, 79
Omission of medial consonants	147
,, words in phrasing	120
On Observation	pages 203 to 206
On Opportunity	pages 206 to 208
P added to *m*	84
P, Omission of	147
Party expressed by intersection	150
Phonetic spelling	1
Phonographic Alphabet	page 189
Phraseograms, List of	pages 191 to 194
Phraseography	29
Phraseogram defined	29
Phrasing, Circles *s, sw,* and *ss* in	48
,, Doubling Principle in	116
,, Halving Principle in	103
,, Injudicious	121
,, Omission of *con* in	page 142
,, ,, words in	120

Pl and *pr* series, Vocalization of .. .. 117 to 119
Position, First 13
  ,,   Second 7
  ,,   Third 18
  ,,   First upright or slanting letter to occupy 18
  ,,   How affected by diphthongs .. 25 to 27
  ,,   of double-length strokes 115
  ,,   ,, half-length strokes 102
  ,,   Short and long vowels equally affect .. 23
  ,,   When unnecessary to observe 152
Prefixes .. .. 132 to 139
Punctuation 8
Quotations, etc. .. .. page 213
R added to *l* and *r* 84
  ,, ,, ,, *mp* by doubling 110
  ,, hook to curved consonants 62
  ,, ,, ,, straight 59
  ,, Half-length upward, not to stand alone 107
  ,, Upward and downward 15, 49, 75, 96
rd and *rt*, Final 107
Railroad expressed by intersection 150
Reference Marks .. .. page 213
Rer, Compound Consonant 84
  ,, ,, ,, cannot be halved .. 106
S, Stroke, when written .. .. .. 52 to 54
Self-, Prefix 136
Sermon Reporting, Indication of Text .. page 214
Sh, how written 11
-ship, Suffix 145
Shn preceded by two vowel signs 83
Shr and *Shl*, how written 63
Shun hook .. .. 78 to 83
Similar words 152
Society expressed by intersection 150
Sound, Student to write according to 1
Speed Practice, Advanced .. .. pages 209 to 212
Suffixes .. .. 140 to 146
T indicated by Halving Principle .. 98 to 107, 119
T, Half-sized, disjoined after *t* or *d* 99
  ,, Omission of 147
There, Compounds of 149
  ,, or *their* indicated by Doubling Principle .. 116
Compounds of 149
Tick *the* 39

INDEX.

Tr, dr, thr indicated by Doubling Principle 108, 109, 112 to 115
-ture   „   „   „   „   111
Vowels, First place long   12
  „ Second „   „   4
  „ Third „   „   17
  „ between two strokes 19, 22
  „ Places of   .. .. 4 to 6
  „ Separate signs for concurring   .. 129, 130
  „ Short   .. .. 20 to 22
  „ Distinguishing..   151
Vowel *aw* joined initially   44
  „ and diphthong, Concurring   130
  „ within *ss* circle 47
  „ cannot be shown between letters expressed by
      loop   51
  „ indication   .. 55, 83, 91, 92, 93, 96, 105
  „ Initial or final, necessitates use of stroke con-
      sonant   .. 50, 74, 85, 86, 101, 112, 126
  „ unaccented short, Omission of   56
W, Abbreviated..   126
W diphthongs ..   .. 122 to 126
-ward, Contraction for   100
-wart,   „   „ 100
word, in phrasing   103
-wort, Contraction   100
would, in phrasing   103
Wh, Compound Consonant   84
Where, Compounds of   149
Whl, Compound Consonant   84
Wl   „   „   84
Y diphthongs   .. .. 122 to 126
-yard, Contraction for   100
Z and *s* circle   .. .. 32 to 37

The Publishers desire to tender their hearty thanks to the large number of American and Canadian teachers and writers of Isaac Pitman's Shorthand who have offered valuable suggestions for the improvement of this work.

www.bookjungle.com *email: sales@bookjungle.com fax: 630-214-0564 mail: Book Jungle PO Box 2226 Champaign, IL 61825*

The Codes Of Hammurabi And Moses
W. W. Davies

QTY

The discovery of the Hammurabi Code is one of the greatest achievements of archaeology, and is of paramount interest, not only to the student of the Bible, but also to all those interested in ancient history...

Religion   **ISBN:** *1-59462-338-4*   Pages:132
MSRP $12.95

The Theory of Moral Sentiments
Adam Smith

QTY

This work from 1749. contains original theories of conscience amd moral judgment and it is the foundation for systemof morals.

Philosophy   **ISBN:** *1-59462-777-0*   Pages:536
MSRP $19.95

Jessica's First Prayer
Hesba Stretton

QTY

In a screened and secluded corner of one of the many railway-bridges which span the streets of London there could be seen a few years ago, from five o'clock every morning until half past eight, a tidily set-out coffee-stall, consisting of a trestle and board, upon which stood two large tin cans, with a small fire of charcoal burning under each so as to keep the coffee boiling during the early hours of the morning when the work-people were thronging into the city on their way to their daily toil...

Childrens   **ISBN:** *1-59462-373-2*   Pages:84
MSRP $9.95

My Life and Work
Henry Ford

QTY

Henry Ford revolutionized the world with his implementation of mass production for the Model T automobile. Gain valuable business insight into his life and work with his own auto-biography... "We have only started on our development of our country we have not as yet, with all our talk of wonderful progress, done more than scratch the surface. The progress has been wonderful enough but..."

Biographies/ **ISBN:** *1-59462-198-5*   Pages:300
MSRP $21.95

www.bookjungle.com email: sales@bookjungle.com fax: 630-214-0564 mail: Book Jungle PO Box 2226 Champaign, IL 61825

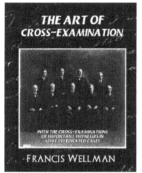

The Art of Cross-Examination
Francis Wellman

QTY

I presume it is the experience of every author, after his first book is published upon an important subject, to be almost overwhelmed with a wealth of ideas and illustrations which could readily have been included in his book, and which to his own mind, at least, seem to make a second edition inevitable. Such certainly was the case with me; and when the first edition had reached its sixth impression in five months, I rejoiced to learn that it seemed to my publishers that the book had met with a sufficiently favorable reception to justify a second and considerably enlarged edition. ..

Reference   ISBN: *1-59462-647-2*   Pages:412   MSRP *$19.95*

On the Duty of Civil Disobedience
Henry David Thoreau

QTY

Thoreau wrote his famous essay, On the Duty of Civil Disobedience, as a protest against an unjust but popular war and the immoral but popular institution of slave-owning. He did more than write—he declined to pay his taxes, and was hauled off to gaol in consequence. Who can say how much this refusal of his hastened the end of the war and of slavery ?

Law   ISBN: *1-59462-747-9*   Pages:48   MSRP *$7.45*

Dream Psychology Psychoanalysis for Beginners
Sigmund Freud

QTY

Sigmund Freud, born Sigismund Schlomo Freud (May 6, 1856 - September 23, 1939), was a Jewish-Austrian neurologist and psychiatrist who co-founded the psychoanalytic school of psychology. Freud is best known for his theories of the unconscious mind, especially involving the mechanism of repression; his redefinition of sexual desire as mobile and directed towards a wide variety of objects; and his therapeutic techniques, especially his understanding of transference in the therapeutic relationship and the presumed value of dreams as sources of insight into unconscious desires.

Psychology   ISBN: *1-59462-905-6*   Pages:196   MSRP *$15.45*

The Miracle of Right Thought
Orison Swett Marden

QTY

Believe with all of your heart that you will do what you were made to do. When the mind has once formed the habit of holding cheerful, happy, prosperous pictures, it will not be easy to form the opposite habit. It does not matter how improbable or how far away this realization may see, or how dark the prospects may be, if we visualize them as best we can, as vividly as possible, hold tenaciously to them and vigorously struggle to attain them, they will gradually become actualized, realized in the life. But a desire, a longing without endeavor, a yearning abandoned or held indifferently will vanish without realization.

Self Help   ISBN: *1-59462-644-8*   Pages:360   MSRP *$25.45* www.bookjungle.com *email: sales@bookjungle.com fax: 630-214-0564 mail: Book Jungle PO Box 2226 Champaign, IL 61825*

QTY

☐ **The Rosicrucian Cosmo-Conception Mystic Christianity** *by Max Heindel*   ISBN: *1-59462-188-8*   **$38.95**
The Rosicrucian Cosmo-conception is not dogmatic, neither does it appeal to any other authority than the reason of the student. It is: not controversial, but is: sent forth in the, hope that it may help to clear...
New Age/Religion Pages 646

☐ **Abandonment To Divine Providence** *by Jean-Pierre de Caussade*   ISBN: *1-59462-228-0*   **$25.95**
"The Rev. Jean Pierre de Caussade was one of the most remarkable spiritual writers of the Society of Jesus in France in the 18th Century. His death took place at Toulouse in 1751. His works have gone through many editions and have been republished...
Inspirational/Religion Pages 400

☐ **Mental Chemistry** *by Charles Haanel*   ISBN: *1-59462-192-6*   **$23.95**
Mental Chemistry allows the change of material conditions by combining and appropriately utilizing the power of the mind. Much like applied chemistry creates something new and unique out of careful combinations of chemicals the mastery of mental chemistry...
New Age Pages 354

☐ **The Letters of Robert Browning and Elizabeth Barret Barrett 1845-1846 vol II**   ISBN: *1-59462-193-4*   **$35.95**
by Robert Browning and Elizabeth Barrett
Biographies Pages 596

☐ **Gleanings In Genesis (volume I)** *by Arthur W. Pink*   ISBN: *1-59462-130-6*   **$27.45**
Appropriately has Genesis been termed "the seed plot of the Bible" for in it we have, in germ form, almost all of the great doctrines which are afterwards fully developed in the books of Scripture which follow...
Religion/Inspirational Pages 420

☐ **The Master Key** *by L. W. de Laurence*   ISBN: *1-59462-001-6*   **$30.95**
In no branch of human knowledge has there been a more lively increase of the spirit of research during the past few years than in the study of Psychology, Concentration and Mental Discipline. The requests for authentic lessons in Thought Control, Mental Discipline and...
New Age/Business Pages 422

☐ **The Lesser Key Of Solomon Goetia** *by L. W. de Laurence*   ISBN: *1-59462-092-X*   **$9.95**
This translation of the first book of the "Lernegton" which is now for the first time made accessible to students of Talismanic Magic was done, after careful collation and edition, from numerous Ancient Manuscripts in Hebrew, Latin, and French...
New Age/Occult Pages 92

☐ **Rubaiyat Of Omar Khayyam** *by Edward Fitzgerald*   ISBN: *1-59462-332-5*   **$13.95**
Edward Fitzgerald, whom the world has already learned, in spite of his own efforts to remain within the shadow of anonymity, to look upon as one of the rarest poets of the century, was born at Bredfield, in Suffolk, on the 31st of March, 1809. He was the third son of John Purcell...
Music Pages 172

☐ **Ancient Law** *by Henry Maine*   ISBN: *1-59462-128-4*   **$29.95**
The chief object of the following pages is to indicate some of the earliest ideas of mankind, as they are reflected in Ancient Law, and to point out the relation of those ideas to modern thought.
Religion/History Pages 452

☐ **Far-Away Stories** *by William J. Locke*   ISBN: *1-59462-129-2*   **$19.45**
"Good wine needs no bush, but a collection of mixed vintages does. And this book is just such a collection. Some of the stories I do not want to remain buried for ever in the museum files of dead magazine-numbers an author's not unpardonable vanity..."
Fiction Pages 272

☐ **Life of David Crockett** *by David Crockett*   ISBN: *1-59462-250-7*   **$27.45**
"Colonel David Crockett was one of the most remarkable men of the times in which he lived. Born in humble life, but gifted with a strong will, an indomitable courage, and unremitting perseverance...
Biographies/New Age Pages 424

☐ **Lip-Reading** *by Edward Nitchie*   ISBN: *1-59462-206-X*   **$25.95**
Edward B. Nitchie, founder of the New York School for the Hard of Hearing, now the Nitchie School of Lip-Reading, Inc, wrote "LIP-READING Principles and Practice". The development and perfecting of this meritorious work on lip-reading was an undertaking...
How-to Pages 400

☐ **A Handbook of Suggestive Therapeutics, Applied Hypnotism, Psychic Science**   ISBN: *1-59462-214-0*   **$24.95**
by Henry Munro
Health/New Age/Health/Self-help Pages 376

☐ **A Doll's House: and Two Other Plays** *by Henrik Ibsen*   ISBN: *1-59462-112-8*   **$19.95**
Henrik Ibsen created this classic when in revolutionary 1848 Rome. Introducing some striking concepts in playwriting for the realist genre, this play has been studied the world over.
Fiction/Classics/Plays 308

☐ **The Light of Asia** *by sir Edwin Arnold*   ISBN: *1-59462-204-3*   **$13.95**
In this poetic masterpiece, Edwin Arnold describes the life and teachings of Buddha. The man who was to become known as Buddha to the world was born as Prince Gautama of India but he rejected the worldly riches and abandoned the reigns of power when...
Religion/History/Biographies Pages 170

☐ **The Complete Works of Guy de Maupassant** *by Guy de Maupassant*   ISBN: *1-59462-157-8*   **$16.95**
"For days and days, nights and nights, I had dreamed of that first kiss which was to consecrate our engagement, and I knew not on what spot I should put my lips..."
Fiction/Classics Pages 240

☐ **The Art of Cross-Examination** *by Francis L. Wellman*   ISBN: *1-59462-309-0*   **$26.95**
Written by a renowned trial lawyer, Wellman imparts his experience and uses case studies to explain how to use psychology to extract desired information through questioning.
How-to/Science/Reference Pages 408

☐ **Answered or Unanswered?** *by Louisa Vaughan*   ISBN: *1-59462-248-5*   **$10.95**
Miracles of Faith in China
Religion Pages 112

☐ **The Edinburgh Lectures on Mental Science (1909)** *by Thomas*   ISBN: *1-59462-008-3*   **$11.95**
This book contains the substance of a course of lectures recently given by the writer in the Queen Street Hail, Edinburgh. Its purpose is to indicate the Natural Principles governing the relation between Mental Action and Material Conditions...
New Age/Psychology Pages 148

☐ **Ayesha** *by H. Rider Haggard*   ISBN: *1-59462-301-5*   **$24.95**
Verily and indeed it is the unexpected that happens! Probably if there was one person upon the earth from whom the Editor of this, and of a certain previous history, did not expect to hear again...
Classics Pages 380

☐ **Ayala's Angel** *by Anthony Trollope*   ISBN: *1-59462-352-X*   **$29.95**
The two girls were both pretty, but Lucy who was twenty-one who supposed to be simple and comparatively unattractive, whereas Ayala was credited, as her Bombwhat romantic name might show, with poetic charm and a taste for romance. Ayala when her father died was nineteen...
Fiction Pages 484

☐ **The American Commonwealth** *by James Bryce*   ISBN: *1-59462-286-8*   **$34.45**
An interpretation of American democratic political theory. It examines political mechanics and society from the perspective of Scotsman James Bryce
Politics Pages 572

☐ **Stories of the Pilgrims** *by Margaret P. Pumphrey*   ISBN: *1-59462-116-0*   **$17.95**
This book explores pilgrims religious oppression in England as well as their escape to Holland and eventual crossing to America on the Mayflower, and their early days in New England...
History Pages 268

www.bookjungle.com email: sales@bookjungle.com fax: 630-214-0564 mail: Book Jungle PO Box 2226 Champaign, IL 61825

Title	ISBN	Price	QTY
The Fasting Cure *by Sinclair Upton* — In the Cosmopolitan Magazine for May, 1910, and in the Contemporary Review (London) for April, 1910, I published an article dealing with my experiences in fasting. I have written a great many magazine articles, but never one which attracted so much attention... *New Age/Self Help/Health Pages 164*	1-59462-222-1	$13.95	☐
Hebrew Astrology *by Sepharial* — In these days of advanced thinking it is a matter of common observation that we have left many of the old landmarks behind and that we are now pressing forward to greater heights and to a wider horizon than that which represented the mind-content of our progenitors... *Astrology Pages 144*	1-59462-308-2	$13.45	☐
Thought Vibration or The Law of Attraction in the Thought World *by William Walker Atkinson* — *Psychology/Religion Pages 144*	1-59462-127-6	$12.95	☐
Optimism *by Helen Keller* — Helen Keller was blind, deaf, and mute since 19 months old, yet famously learned how to overcome these handicaps, communicate with the world, and spread her lectures promoting optimism. An inspiring read for everyone... *Biographies/Inspirational Pages 84*	1-59462-108-X	$15.95	☐
Sara Crewe *by Frances Burnett* — In the first place, Miss Minchin lived in London. Her home was a large, dull, tall one, in a large, dull square, where all the houses were alike, and all the sparrows were alike, and where all the door-knockers made the same heavy sound... *Childrens/Classic Pages 88*	1-59462-360-0	$9.45	☐
The Autobiography of Benjamin Franklin *by Benjamin Franklin* — The Autobiography of Benjamin Franklin has probably been more extensively read than any other American historical work, and no other book of its kind has had such ups and downs of fortune. Franklin lived for many years in England, where he was agent... *Biographies/History Pages 332*	1-59462-135-7	$24.95	☐

Name	
Email	
Telephone	
Address	
City, State ZIP	

☐ Credit Card   ☐ Check / Money Order

Credit Card Number	
Expiration Date	
Signature	

Please Mail to: Book Jungle
                    PO Box 2226
                    Champaign, IL 61825
or Fax to: 630-214-0564

ORDERING INFORMATION
web: *www.bookjungle.com*
email: *sales@bookjungle.com*
fax: *630-214-0564*
mail: *Book Jungle PO Box 2226 Champaign, IL 61825*
or PayPal *to sales@bookjungle.com*

Please contact us for bulk discounts

DIRECT-ORDER TERMS

20% Discount if You Order Two or More Books
Free Domestic Shipping!
Accepted: Master Card, Visa, Discover, American Express

Lightning Source UK Ltd.
Milton Keynes UK
UKOW07f1904060315

247431UK00004B/205/P